Life Changing Daily Devotions

Lolita' M. Jones

Life Changers, LLC

FOREWORD BY BISHOP CARL D. HODGES

Printed in the United States of America

FOREWORD

Regardless of a person's station in life, encouragement always helps and every one of us finds ourselves in need of encouragement from time to time. Job 14:1 declares "Man that is born of a woman is of few days and full of trouble." The Message Bible expresses it another way. "We're all adrift in the same boat: too few days, too many troubles." With just a few days on earth, we are destined to encounter trouble, heartache, disappointment, grief, and the list goes on. Making it through these times requires a timely *word* to help us out of a slump; to pull us up from the doldrums; and re-orient our steps. For this reason, God has called Evangelist Lolita Jones to the body of Christ.

It is faith in God's word that will guarantee that we live on top. And God has inspired Lolita to compile a collection of devotions to, not only lift us by encouraging us, but to also push us towards our various destinies.

I have no doubt that the Holy Spirit has inspired the words and phrases contained in this book. The words from the Sprit have flowed from Lolita's heart, onto the pages of this book. And now, these words are ready to leap into our hearts. The devotions in this book will serve as a ready companion to your Bible helping you to discern God's will and His ways.

Rather than recapitulate the same old stories, or settle for the usual feel-good collection of poems, and epithets, Evangelist Jones challenges the reader to reach for higher and greater. The devotions in this book, when considered in faith, holler at the reader, "You have no choice but to succeed!" This book says that in spite of the many vicissitudes of life and the inevitable hurts and disappointments that come simply because we are card-carrying members of the human race, God is on our side; He is for us; and we will win!

The devotions Lolita has collected are the result of walking with and listening to the Lord in dry places. I mean literally dry places such as the desert of the Middle East while serving as a Soldier in the U. S. Navy. The Holy Spirit spoke to and conditioned her heart on *the back side of that desert.* God revealed Himself as the all-knowing, all-powerful, everywhere-at-the-same-time God of divine love and providence that we see portrayed in the Bible. In this book, Lolita shares those joyous experiences with us. The reader who looks to God in hope, or simply looks for hope, will find that this book will affirm his relationship with God; challenge his faith for living; direct her path; raise her expectations for life; and inspire enduring faith. Whether you read one page, multiple pages, or the whole book at once, you will leave this book convinced victory is an available option regardless of your circumstances. This book will surely be included in my personal tool chest of ministry helps.

Bishop Carl D. Hodges
Prelate, Japan Jurisdiction
Church of God in Christ, Inc.

"Lolita' has poured her heart and soul into every daily inspiration and scripture that is penned. An invaluable and insightful work that will challenge every reader to seek God and challenge the inner man. Her inspirations are for both young and mature Christians in Christ. She has truly sought the wisdom of God."

--David Brent, Associate Elder at Cathedral of Faith COGIC

USN, Retired

INTRODUCTION

It is perhaps not a considerable stretch to believe that every day, people across the world are inundated with perceived negative influencers. These negative influencers can be presented in countless ways (e.g. mass communication mediums, family members, work/social associates, books, magazines, etc.), and the ways in which they may impact the decision making and actions of an individual, are unique to each person. If a person is not careful, adherence to and acceptance of negative influences can result in a host of debilitating outcomes including depression, anxiety disorders, panic attacks, a range of illnesses, or worst-case death. Based upon perception, fortunately or unfortunately, we are what we think.

Formally defined in textbooks, thinking involves manipulating information mentally by forming concepts, solving problems, making decisions, and reflecting in a critical or creative manner. With emphasis on the importance of making decisions and the significant impacts that may incur from decisions made, this easy to read and transport book provides you with short, well thought out, and spiritually guided words of encouragement to help counteract the otherwise debilitating effects of negative influencers. It is lovingly recommended that each theme oriented write-up be used as a primary source for daily devotions.

The devotions shared in this book have helped me and I pray that it will be a source of inspiration for you as well. Instead of allowing your mind to be saturated by negative influencers, adhere to the guidance found in Philippians 4:8 - Finally, brethren, whatsoever things are true, whatsoever things are honest, whatsoever things are just, whatsoever things are pure, whatsoever things are lovely, whatsoever things are of good report; if there be any virtue, and if there be any praise, think on these things. Finally, as you read these devotions, remain ever mindful that in accordance with 2 Timothy 3:16 & 17 - All scripture is given by inspiration of God, and is profitable for doctrine, for reproof, for correction, for instruction in righteousness: 17 That the man of God may be perfect, thoroughly furnished unto all good works. Enjoy the devotions and I bid you Godspeed!

Humbly Submitted,

Dr. Nicholas M. Anthony Jr., Ph.D.
USA, Retired

MY PURPOSE

To equip (prepare) his (God's) people for works of service, so that the body of Christ may be built up until we all reach unity in the faith and in the knowledge of the Son of God and become mature, attaining to the whole measure of the fullness of Christ.   Ephesians 4:12-13 NIV

MY FAITH CONFESSION

I have the mind of Jesus Christ,

I am the image of GOD,

HIS Word is filled with

Power, Grace, and Love.

I receive what God has for me

and Transformation is on His menu.

So therefore,

I am Renewed
I am Whole
I am Healed
I am Delivered
I am Favored

And it is so. In Jesus Christ. Amen

BE STRONG IN THE FAITH!

Stay alert! Watch out for your great enemy, the devil. He prowls around like a roaring lion, looking for someone to devour. Stand firm against him, and be strong in your faith. Remember that your family of believers all over the world is going through the same kind of suffering you are. In His kindness God called you to share in His eternal glory by means of Christ Jesus. So after you have suffered a little while, He will restore, support, and strengthen you, and He will place you on a firm foundation.   1 Peter 5:8-10 NLT

SING! SING! SING A NEW SONG!

Psalm 33:3
Sing unto him a new song; play skillfully with a loud noise.

Psalm 40:3 NLT
He has given me a new song to sing, a hymn of praise to our God. Many will see what he has done and be amazed. They will put their trust in the LORD.

Psalm 96:1 NLT
Sing a new song to the LORD! Let the whole earth sing to the LORD!

Psalm 98:1 NLT
Sing a new song to the LORD, for he has done wonderful deeds. His right hand has won a mighty victory; his holy arm has shown his saving power!

Psalm 144:9 NLT
I will sing a new song to you, O God! I will sing your praises with a ten-stringed harp.

Psalm 149:1 NLT
Praise the LORD! Sing to the LORD a new song. Sing his praises in the assembly of the faithful.

Isaiah 42:10,12 NLT
Sing a new song to the LORD! Sing his praises from the ends of the earth! Sing, all you who sail the seas, all you who live in distant coastlands. Let the whole world glorify the LORD; let it sing his praise.

Put a song in your spirit and in your mouth. Now sing a new song unto the Lord for He is GOOD!!!

TAKE THE LIMITS OFF. DON'T LIMIT GOD.

Psalm 78:41 says that the children of Israel limited the Lord because they did not remember His power (verse 42). We free God's Hand to bless when we remember His previous blessings. Psalm 103:2 says to remember His blessings.

EXPECT! Never underestimate the power of expectation. Expect God's power to strengthen you today. Expect to be led by His Spirit. We limit what God can do in our lives when we lower our expectations.

John 1:16 NLT
From his abundance we have all received one gracious blessing after another.

2 Corinthians 9:8 NIV
And God is able to bless you abundantly, so that in all things at all times, having all that you need, you will abound in every good work.

Philippians 4:6-7 NLT
Don't worry about anything; instead, pray about everything. Tell God what you need, and thank him for all he has done. Then you will experience God's peace, which exceeds anything we can understand. His peace will guard your hearts and minds as you live in Christ Jesus.

Take the limits off, and expect miracles right now in your life.

I'M PRAYING FOR YOU

I have not stopped thanking God for you. I pray for you
constantly, asking God, the glorious Father of our Lord Jesus
Christ, to give you spiritual wisdom and insight so that you
might grow in your knowledge of God. I pray that your hearts
will be flooded with light so that you can understand the
confident hope He has given to those He called-His holy
people who are His rich and glorious inheritance. I also pray
that you will understand the incredible greatness of God's
power for us who believe Him. This is the same mighty power
that raised Christ from the dead and seated Him in the place of
honor at God's right hand in the heavenly realms.
Ephesians 1:16-20 NLT

And it is so. In Jesus Christ I pray. Amen.

DO YOU WANT THE LAST WORD OR DO YOU WANT GOD'S BLESSING?

Be encouraged. That person may have hurt you, talked bad about you, or set you up for failure but stand on the WORD of God. Jesus told us to turn the other cheek (Matthew 5:39). Don't give them a piece of your mind but rather give them to God. Let God handle it His way.

Romans 12:19 (NLT) says, "Dear friends, never take revenge. Leave that to the righteous anger of God. For the Scriptures say, "I will take revenge; I will pay them back," says the LORD."

David said in Psalm 23:5 (Voice), "You spread out a table before me, provisions in the midst of attack from my enemies; You care for all my needs, anointing my head with soothing, fragrant oil, filling my cup again and again with Your grace."

No matter what the people (enemy) send your direction to hurt or stop you, don't have the last word. Give them to GOD!!!

Joseph said, "You intended to harm me, but God intended it all for good............" (Genesis 50:20 NLT).

Let God Almighty bless you beyond your imagination in front of ALL your enemies.

Vengeance is mine; I will repay, saith the Lord.

Don't Settle for Good Enough

For I know what I have planned for you,' says the LORD. 'I have plans to prosper you, not to harm you. I have plans to give you a future filled with hope. Jeremiah 29:11 NET

In Genesis chapter 11, Terah, Abraham's father was the original one that departed out of Ur, which was a land of idolatry. Terah departed with his sons and daughters in law, and Lot (his son Haran's child) and they were going to the land of Canaan. But something happened!!!! Terah's baby boy, Haran, died. Terah was so hurt and distracted that he settled for good enough. He stopped the journey and settled in a land that he named after his son, Haran.

Saints, it's dangerous to settle for good enough. Terah settled and the Bible says, "Terah lived for 205 years and died while still in Haran" (Genesis 11:32 NLT).

God may have given you a vision or sent the prophet to give you a word, and that blessing, miracle, healing, or deliverance haven't manifested in the natural as of yet BUT don't you settle. Jesus said, "Simon, Simon, behold, Satan hath desired to have you, that he may sift you as wheat: But I have prayed for thee, that thy faith fail not: and when thou art converted, strengthen thy brethren" (Luke 22:31-32).

Don't settle, my sister. Don't settle, my brother.

God has a plan to do superabundantly, far over and above

all that we [dare] ask or think [infinitely beyond our highest prayers, desires, thoughts, hopes, or dreams]— Ephesians 3:20 AMP. But we can't settle.

David said, "Wait on the Lord: be of good courage, and he shall strengthen thine heart: wait, I say, on the Lord" (Psalm 27:14).

But they that wait upon the Lord shall renew their strength; they shall mount up with wings as eagles; they shall run, and not be weary; and they shall walk, and not faint.
   Isaiah 40:31

DO NOT SETTLE. GOD HAS GREATNESS IN YOUR DESTINY

ASK BIG

Now Jabez called on the God of Israel, saying, "Oh that You would bless me indeed and enlarge my border, and that Your hand might be with me, and that You would keep me from harm that it may not pain me!" And God granted him what he requested. 1 Chronicles 4:10 NASB

We read multiple times in the Bible, how Great and Awesome God is. Abraham, Moses, Hannah, Elisha, Elijah, King David, King Hezekiah, and many others asked God for Big things. They asked God for the impossible. And God went beyond their dreams, goals, and thoughts.

But Jabez, a young man whose name means "to bare in sorrow". This was the first and only time he was mentioned in the Bible (1 Chronicles 4:9-10). He had the audacity to ask BIG and his faith backed it up. And the Bible says, "And God granted him what he requested".

What would happen if you stepped out in faith and asked BIG? Do you need a financial miracle? Ask God Almighty.
In His Kingdom, He used Solid GOLD to make the streets. So that let me know Our God thinks big. Apostle Paul told us that we have the mind of Jesus Christ. (1 Corinthians 2:16) So we must think Big like Christ.

Pray like Jabez and expect to receive superabundantly, far over and above all that you [dare] ask or think [infinitely beyond your highest prayers, desires, thoughts, hopes, or dreams]— Ephesians 3:20 Amp

Ask BIG.

The MASTER'S Touch

Matthew 8:3
And Jesus put forth his hand, and touched him, ... And immediately his leprosy was cleansed.

Matthew 8:15
And he touched her hand, and the fever left her: and she arose, and ministered unto them.

Matthew 9:29-30
Then touched he their eyes, saying, According to your faith be it unto you. And their eyes were opened; ....

Matthew 20:34
So Jesus had compassion on them , and touched their eyes: and immediately their eyes received sight, and they followed him.

There are many scriptures that talks about Jesus' touch. Today, our Lord and Savior is sitting on the right hand of God our Father (Ephesians 1:20) but we have His Word. Jesus said, "He that believeth on me, as the scripture hath said, out of his belly shall flow rivers of living water" (John 7:38).

Do you need a touch from the Master? Worship Him. Praise Him. Call out to Him. Tell Him what you need. Just one touch from the Master will change everything.

Jesus said, "........., I am come that they might have life, and that they might have it more abundantly" (John 10:10).

Let the Master touch you. Let Him touch your marriage. Let Him touch your family. Let Him touch your finances. No matter what it is, let the Master touch it.

Father God in Jesus Christ, stretch forth Your hand and touch my body, my children, my spouse, my finances, and the ministry. I receive all that You have for me. So I declare and believe I am healed, whole, restored, blessed, delivered, free, and favored, in Jesus' Name. And it is so. Amen.

I'M WAITING BUT I'M PRAISING

Isaiah 40:31 AMPC
But those who wait for the Lord who expect, look for, and hope in Him shall change and renew their strength and power; they shall lift their wings and mount up close to God as eagles mount up to the sun; they shall run and not be weary, they shall walk and not faint or become tired.

Are you waiting for the Lord to do something great in Your Life?

Did God make you a Promise and you waiting for the manifestation?

Don't let your waiting be in vain.

I remember when my children were younger, and I would take them to their medical appointments. We always arrived 30 minutes early. But while waiting my children would play with the toys and I would read a magazine. It seemed as though once we occupied ourselves, the wait time sped up.

What would happen if you started praising God while waiting on that break-through?

Psalm 27:14
Wait on the Lord: be of good courage, and he shall strengthen thine heart: wait, I say, on the Lord.

While waiting, Paul and Silas prayed and praised. And you know what happened.

And suddenly there was a great earthquake, so that the foundations of the prison were shaken: and immediately all the doors were opened, and every one's bands were loosed.
Acts 16:26

David said, "My soul, wait thou only upon God; for my expectation is from him" (Psalm 62:5).

Are you expecting anything from God?

Open your mouth and praise Him.

Psalm 9:2
I will be glad and rejoice in thee: I will sing praise to thy name, O thou most High.

I AM HERE

Isaiah 43:2-3
When thou passest through the waters, I will be with thee; and through the rivers, they shall not overflow thee: when thou walkest through the fire, thou shalt not be burned; neither shall the flame kindle upon thee. For I am the Lord thy God, the Holy One of Israel, thy Saviour.

Why do you worry my child? I AM here. Tell me all about it. I AM listening.

Hebrews 13:5b AMP
For He [God] Himself has said, "I will not in any way fail you nor give you up nor leave you without support. [I will] not, [I will] not, [I will] not in any degree leave you helpless nor forsake nor let [you] down (relax My hold on you)!"

This word is for you. No matter what you're going through, God Almighty is with you. Things may look a little dim but God Almighty is with you.

You've prayed and cried, and prayed and cried but you are still standing because God Almighty brought you through.

This is a word from God Yeshua for you. You will make it. This test will make you stronger. You will be wiser. I AM with you. I AM carrying you through this. I AM here for you, My child.

Lamentations 3:22 AMPC
It is because of the Lord's mercy and loving-kindness that we are not consumed, because His tender compassions fail not.

I AM here

TRANSFORM

Romans 12:1-2
I beseech you therefore, brethren, by the mercies of God, that ye present your bodies a living sacrifice, holy, acceptable unto God, which is your reasonable service.
And be not conformed to this world: but be ye transformed by the renewing of your mind, that ye may prove what is that good, and acceptable, and perfect, will of God.

Did you know when you transform your mind, you also transform your world. Evangelist, how do I transform my world? Well, let me share with you.

When you allow God's word to take root in you and perform that which God desires, you set yourself up for BLESSINGS, FAVOR, HEALING, and TRANSFORMATION.
This world is filled with darkness, doubt, hatred, fear, sickness, and disease but when you allow God's Word to transform your mind, you become a solution in this world.
You begin to see with your physical and spiritual eye. Then you can pray God's Word over people, neighborhoods, cities, states, and nations. When you pray, Heaven is backing you, and transformation begins.

Jesus said in Matthew 5:14,16, "Ye are the light of the world. A city that is set on an hill cannot be hid. Let your light so shine before men, that they may see your good works, and glorify your Father which is in heaven."

Psalm 33:12
Blessed is the nation whose God is the Lord........

Let transformation begin with you.

ENCOURAGE OTHERS

Philippians 2:1 NLT
Is there any encouragement from belonging to Christ? Any
comfort from his love? Any fellowship together in the Spirit?
Are your hearts tender and compassionate?

When was the last time you encouraged someone in the faith?
In the above scripture, Apostle Paul was asking the Philippine
church to encourage one another by having the attitude of
Jesus Christ.

Apostle Peter encouraged the saints in 1 Peter 5, to cast their
cares upon the Lord. And that there were believers across the
nations that were also going through hard times but be
encouraged. In his closing, he said, "I have written and sent
this short letter to you with the help of Silas, whom I
commend to you as a faithful brother. My purpose in writing is
to encourage you and assure you that what you are
experiencing is truly part of God's grace for you. Stand firm in
this grace" (1 Peter 5:12 NLT).

God has anointed us to be Kingdom builders. In Ephesians 4,
Apostle Paul told the five-fold ministry in verses 12-13 that
Jesus gave these offices, "for the equipping of the saints for the
work of service, to the building up of the body of Christ; until
we all attain to the unity of the faith, and of the knowledge of
the Son of God, to a mature man, to the measure of the stature
which belongs to the fullness of Christ" (Ephesians 4:12-13
NASB).

How do we build up the body of Christ? By encouraging our
sisters and brothers in the faith through the Word of God.

Find someone today, that you can encourage. Many believers
hide behind a smile but are broken and depressed inside. Ask
God Holy Spirit to give you a word for those that are going
through.

Isaiah 50:4 AMPC
The Lord God has given Me the tongue of a disciple and of one who is taught, that I should know how to speak a word in season to him who is weary. He wakens Me morning by morning, He wakens My ear to hear as a disciple as one who is taught.

Encourage them until they are one in faith, believing God for the impossible. Remember faith cometh by hearing and hearing by the Word of God.
Use God's Word to encourage because His Word can't fail.

SING YOUR WAY TO VICTORY

2 Chronicles 20:21-22 AMPC
When he (Jehoshaphat) had consulted with the people, he appointed singers to sing to the Lord and praise Him in their holy priestly garments as they went out before the army, saying, Give thanks to the Lord, for His mercy and loving-kindness endure forever.
And when they began to sing and to praise, the Lord set ambushments against the men of Ammon, Moab, and Mount Seir who had come against Judah, and they were self-slaughtered;

When we sing unto our Lord God, it confuses the enemy. Singing is a weapon (Acts 16:15-16). When we sing to God, evil spirits got to leave (1 Samuel 16:23).

Sing! Sing! Sing! Give thanks to the Lord, for His mercy and loving-kindness endure forever.

SHOUT UNTO GOD ALMIGHTY

Joshua 6:16,20
And it came to pass at the seventh time, when the priests blew with the trumpets, Joshua said unto the people, Shout; for the Lord hath given you the city. So the people shouted when the priests blew with the trumpets: and it came to pass, when the people heard the sound of the trumpet, and the people shouted with a great shout, that the wall fell down flat, so that the people went up into the city, every man straight before him, and they took the city.

Psalm 47:1
O clap your hands, all ye people; shout unto God with the voice of triumph.

Many raise their voices to shout to their child. But how many of us raise our voices to shout unto God?

In the Hebrew SHABACH is shout which means a great blast, battle cry, to cry out, to sound an alarm, a way to express worship, to command, to triumph.

Throughout the Old Testament when the prophet told the people to SHOUT, their enemies were destroyed, blessings saturated them, and walls fell flat.

Imagine this.......The next time trouble knocks on your door, instead of calling your friends, complaining, and getting fearful or depressed, you start shouting praise to God Almighty. Lord I love you. Lord God I trust you. Lord I thank you. Hallelujah. Thank You, Jesus and so on.

King David said in Psalm 5:11-12, "But let all those that put their trust in thee rejoice: let them ever shout for joy, because thou defendest them: let them also that love thy name be joyful in thee. For thou, Lord, wilt bless the righteous; with favour wilt thou compass him as with a shield".

ROOTED, STABLISHED, AND COMPLETE
WE ARE THE TOTAL PACKAGE

Colossians 2:6-7,9-10 NLT
And now, just as you accepted Christ Jesus as your Lord, you must continue to follow him. Let your roots grow down into him, and let your lives be built on him. Then your faith will grow strong in the truth you were taught, and you will overflow with thankfulness. For in Christ lives all the fullness of God in a human body. So you also are complete through your union with Christ, who is the head over every ruler and authority.

In this world, so many people are looking for the total package. The total package in their eyes are, a six-figure salary, a big beautiful house, an Ivy League education, the bling, and good looks.
But we, the believers are the total package because of Jesus Christ our Lord and Savior. We are rooted in Jesus Christ, stablished in Him, and are complete. We have no need to run after things of this world because Jesus Christ said in
John 14:13-14 NLT, "You can ask for anything in my name, and I will do it, so that the Son can bring glory to the Father. Yes, ask me for anything in my name, and I will do it!"

We are the total package. We don't have to make anything happen. We don't have to toil. Whatsoever we do prospers and succeed (Psalm 1:3b).

Encourage yourself and declare over your life; I AM THE TOTAL PACKAGE. I am rooted, stablished, and complete. And it is so. In JESUS Christ.

TRUST IN ME

Isaiah 26:3-4 NLT
You will keep in perfect peace all who trust in you, all whose thoughts are fixed on you! Trust in the LORD always, for the LORD GOD is the eternal Rock.

Genesis 49:18 NLT
I trust in you for salvation, O LORD!

Psalm 25:1-2 NLT
O LORD, I give my life to you. I trust in you, my God! Do not let me be disgraced, or let my enemies rejoice in my defeat.

Proverbs 3:5 NLT
Trust in the LORD with all your heart; do not depend on your own understanding.

Isaiah 12:2 NLT
See, God has come to save me. I will trust in him and not be afraid. The LORD GOD is my strength and my song; he has given me victory."

Jeremiah 29:11-12 NET
[For I know what I have planned for you,' says the LORD. 'I have plans to prosper you, not to harm you. I have plans to give you a future filled with hope. When you call out to me and come to me in prayer, I will hear your prayers.

HE'S WITH YOU

.............I see that the LORD is always with me. I will not be shaken, for he is right beside me. No wonder my heart is glad, and my tongue shouts his praises! My body rests in hope. For you will not leave my soul among the dead or allow your Holy One to rot in the grave. You have shown me the way of life, and you will fill me with the joy of your presence. Acts 2:25-28 NLT

GOD DELIGHTS IN YOU

Zephaniah 3:17 NLT
For the LORD your God is living among you. He is a mighty savior. He will take delight in you with gladness. With His love, He will calm all your fears. He will rejoice over you with joyful songs.

Psalm 18:19 NLT
He led me to a place of safety; He rescued me because He delights in me.

Psalm 37:23 NLT
The LORD directs the steps of the godly. He delights in every detail of their lives.

Psalm 147:11 NLT
.........the LORD's delight is in those who fear Him, those who put their hope in His unfailing love.

Psalm 149:4 NLT
For the LORD delights in His people; He crowns the humble with victory.

Just imagine, the creator of everything delights in you. God takes delight (pleasure, joy) in you. Rejoice!!! Rejoice!!!! Rejoice in knowing God Almighty delights in you and you can't change His mind.

FILLED WITH AWE

Habakkuk 3:2 NLT
I have heard all about you, LORD. I am filled with awe by your amazing works. In this time of our deep need, help us again as you did in years gone by. And in your anger, remember your mercy.

Habakkuk was a prophet of God in a time when God's people were suffering disgrace and evil seemed to be winning the day. But Habakkuk didn't let the prominent events of his day discourage him. He reminded himself who God was and encouraged himself with memories of the "amazing things" God had accomplished in the past. He acknowledged that God's anger towards his people was justified. He knew, however, that God could save his generation as well as any other, for the Lord was merciful. So he laced his pleas for mercy and salvation with expressions of awe and praise.

In your time of need, let your prayers begin and end with praise for the God who is worthy of all glory and honor.

ANSWER THE DOOR

Revelation 3:20 ESV
Behold, I stand at the door and knock. If anyone hears my
voice and opens the door, I will come in to him and eat with
him, and he with me.

Have you ever had someone knock on your door? I've
discovered only visitors knock but those that have a key, uses
their key to gain entrance.

As believers, we sometime dictate to God and tell Him what we
will give Him. But God want it all. He wants all your heart, all
your problems, all your cares, all your pain......He want it all.

In this scripture Jesus let us know that He's standing at the
door of our heart, knocking. He doesn't want a section,
chamber, or room but he wants the whole Heart. He wants to
be invited into those secret places where we hid the hurt from
a bad relationship. He wants to be invited into those off limit
places of your heart.

Ephesians 3:17
That Christ may dwell in your hearts by faith

Jesus want to reside in the whole heart.

1 Peter 5:7 TLB
Let Him have all your worries and cares, for He is always
thinking about you and watching everything that concerns
you.

Answer the door and invite Him in.

I GOT THE POWER

Acts 1:8 AMPC
But you shall receive power (ability, efficiency, and might) when the Holy Spirit has come upon you, ...

Luke 9:1
Then He called His twelve disciples together, and gave them power and authority over all devils, and to cure diseases.

Luke 4:32 AMPC
And they were amazed at His teaching, for His word was with authority and ability and weight and power.

Luke 10:19 AMPC
Behold! I have given you authority and power to trample upon serpents and scorpions, and physical and mental strength and ability over all the power that the enemy possesses; and nothing shall in any way harm you.

The next time they tell you, you have no power, remember Jesus Christ gave you power before He went to the cross and you received more power after you received God Holy Spirit (Our COMFORTER).

Tell yourself, "I GOT THE POWER"!!!!

I got the power to live pleasingly unto God. I got the authority and power over all devils and to curse disease. I have authority and power to trample upon serpents and scorpions, and physical and mental strength and ability over all the power that the enemy possesses; and nothing shall in any way harm me.

Speak God's Word over every situation and you will see the Power....that same Power that raised Jesus Christ from the dead, lives and breathes in you (Romans 8:11, 9:17).

I GOT THE POWER!!!!

I DECREE AND BELIEVE

May He grant you out of the rich treasury of His glory to be strengthened and reinforced with mighty power in the inner man by God Holy Spirit Himself indwelling your innermost being and personality. May Christ through your faith actually dwell (settle down, abide, make His permanent home) in your hearts! May you be rooted deep in love and founded securely on love, That you may have the power and be strong to apprehend and grasp with all the saints God's devoted people, the experience of that love what is the breadth and length and height and depth of it; That you may really come to know practically, through experience for yourselves the love of Christ, which far surpasses mere knowledge without experience; that you may be filled through all your being unto all the fullness of God may have the richest measure of the divine Presence, and become a body wholly filled and flooded with God Himself!   Ephesians 3:16-19 AMPC

And it is so. In Jesus Christ. So be it.

USE THE KEYS

Matthew 16:19
And I will give unto thee the keys of the kingdom of heaven: and whatsoever thou shalt bind on earth shall be bound in heaven: and whatsoever thou shalt loose on earth shall be loosed in heaven.

John 10:7,9
Then said Jesus unto them again, Verily, verily, I say unto you, I am the door of the sheep. I am the door: by me if any man enter in, he shall be saved, and shall go in and out, and find pasture.

When we became one with Christ, He gave us the keys, not to the kingdom but of the kingdom of Heaven.

In your home, do one key unlock every door in your home??? I hope not. One key unlocks the entry door, another key unlocks your room door, another key unlocks the bathroom door, and another key unlocks the guest room door.

And you have all these keys on your key ring. But you have to know which key to use to gain access to whatever room you want to go in. When you purchased your home you were given keys to the main door and to your mailbox. But you must know which key to use. The same way with the Kingdom of Heaven. We must recognize and learn the keys to access what's stored in Heaven for us.

God Holy Spirit is trying to teach us which key to use to access the doors in Heaven, but we must listen!!!!! Jesus got us in the door but we must take the initiative to learn how to use each key to unlock the divine things in heaven.

Evangelist, how can I do this?

Seek ye first the Kingdom of God and His righteousness, and all these things shall be added unto you (Matthew 6:33).

Matthew 25:34 NLT
Then the King (Jesus) will say to those on his right, 'Come, you who are blessed by my Father, inherit the Kingdom prepared for you from the creation of the world'.

Use the keys

GOD'S BENEFIT PACKAGE
THE SIX FOLD BLESSING

Psalm 103:1-2 NKJV
Bless the LORD, O my soul; And all that is within me, bless
His holy name! Bless the LORD, O my soul, And forget not all
His benefits:
1. Who forgives all your iniquities,
2. Who heals all your diseases,
3. Who redeems your life from destruction,
4. Who crowns you with lovingkindness and tender mercies,
5. Who satisfies your mouth with good things,
6. So that your youth is renewed like the eagle's.

When starting a new job, most companies require you to work
30, 60, or 90 days before the benefits are activated. But God
Almighty is a righteous and just employer. The moment we
receive Jesus Christ as our Lord and Savior, His benefit
package is activated.

After meditating on God's Benefit Package it makes me praise
Him even more. It encourages me that God is thinking about
me.

Psalm 35:27 NKJV
Let them shout for joy and be glad, Who favor my righteous
cause; And let them say continually, "Let the LORD be
magnified, Who has pleasure in the prosperity of His servant."

Enjoy, your benefits.

GIVE THANKS

1 Thessalonians 5:18
In every thing give thanks: for this is the will of God in Christ
Jesus concerning you.

Psalm 18:49
Therefore will I give thanks unto thee, O Lord, among the
heathen, and sing praises unto thy name.

In life we all go through our ups and downs, trials and
tribulations, but we as Believers are encouraged to give thanks
in every thing.

1 Corinthians 15:57
But thanks be to God, which giveth us the victory through our
Lord Jesus Christ.

Psalm 107:21
Oh that men would praise the Lord for his goodness, and for
his wonderful works to the children of men!

Revelation 11:17
......We give thee thanks, O Lord God Almighty, which art, and
wast, and art to come; ....,

Psalm 140:13
Surely the righteous shall give thanks unto thy name: the
upright shall dwell in thy presence.

Psalm 136:26
O give thanks unto the God of heaven: for His mercy endureth
for ever.

Psalm 119:62
At midnight I will rise to give thanks unto thee because of thy
righteous judgments.

Psalm 118:29
O give thanks unto the Lord; for he is good: for his mercy
endureth for ever.

Psalm 97:12
Rejoice in the Lord, ye righteous; and give thanks at the
remembrance of his holiness.

Psalm 75:1
Unto thee, O God, do we give thanks, unto thee do we give
thanks: for that thy name is near thy wondrous works declare.

Before you complain about that job, give thanks to God for
having a source of income. Before you complain about that
car, give thanks to God because you don't have to wait for a
bus. Before you complain about your children, give thanks to
God for children are an inheritance from the Lord.

Take time now and give thanks to God, who always causes you
to triumph, who heals all diseases, who listens to your cry, and
who will never leave you nor forsake you.

GIVE THANKS

WHAT GOD SAYS ABOUT YOUR CHILDREN: THE SEED OF THE RIGHTEOUS

Psalm 112:1-3
Praise ye the Lord. Blessed is the man that feareth the Lord, that delighteth greatly in his commandments. His seed shall be mighty upon earth: the generation of the upright shall be blessed. Wealth and riches shall be in his house: and his righteousness endureth for ever.

Proverbs 11:21
Though hand join in hand, the wicked shall not be unpunished: but the seed of the righteous shall be delivered.

Psalm 90:16 AMPC
Let Your work the signs of Your power be revealed to Your servants, and Your glorious majesty to their children.

Psalm 102:28 AMPC
The children of Your servants shall dwell safely and continue, and their descendants shall be established before You.

Psalm 115:14
The Lord shall increase you more and more, you and your children.

Isaiah 44:3-5 NLT
For I will pour out water to quench your thirst and to irrigate your parched fields. And I will pour out my Spirit on your descendants, and my blessing on your children. They will thrive like watered grass, like willows on a riverbank. Some will proudly claim, 'I belong to the LORD.' Others will say, 'I am a descendant of Jacob.' Some will write the LORD's name on their hands and will take the name of Israel as their own."

Psalm 147:13 AMPC
For He has strengthened and made hard the bars of your gates, and He has blessed your children within you.

Isaiah 49:18 NLT
Look around you and see, for all your children will come back to you. As surely as I live," says the LORD, "they will be like jewels or bridal ornaments for you to display.

Joel 2:28 Voice
Then in those days I will pour My Spirit to all humanity; your children will boldly and prophetically speak the word of God.

God has spoken, therefore you speak it into the lives of your seed.

And it is so. In Jesus Christ. Amen.

TRAIN THEM UP

Psalm 127:3 NLT
Children are a gift from the LORD; they are a reward from him.

1 Samuel 1:27-28 NLT
I asked the LORD to give me this boy, and He has granted my request. Now I am giving him to the LORD, and he will belong to the LORD his whole life." And they worshiped the LORD there.

Proverbs 22:6 TLB
Teach a child to choose the right path, and when he is older, he will remain upon it.

Exodus 35:31 AMPC
And He has filled him with the Spirit of God, with ability and wisdom, with intelligence and understanding, and with knowledge and all craftsmanship.

Daniel 1:17
..........God gave them knowledge and skill in all learning and wisdom: and Daniel had understanding in all visions and dreams.

Acts 7:22
And Moses was learned in all the wisdom of the Egyptians, and was mighty in words and in deeds.

Colossians 4:14
Luke, the beloved physician, ...

Matthew 9:9 NLT
As Jesus was walking along, he saw a man named Matthew sitting at his tax collector's booth. "Follow me and be my disciple," Jesus said to him. So Matthew got up and followed him.

Ephesians 4:11 NLT
Now these are the gifts Christ gave to the church: the apostles, the prophets, the evangelists, and the pastors and teachers.

Give your children to the Lord God, no matter how old or young. God will use them in His service.

Joel 2:28 Voice
Then in those days I will pour My Spirit to all humanity; your children will boldly and prophetically speak the word of God.

Jeremiah 29:11 NIrV
I know the plans I have for you," announces the LORD. "I want you to enjoy success. I do not plan to harm you. I will give you hope for the years to come.

I WILL LAND ON MY FEET

Hebrews 11:1 AMPC
NOW FAITH is the assurance (the confirmation, the title deed) of the things we hope for, being the proof of things we do not see and the conviction of their reality faith perceiving as real fact what is not revealed to the senses.

Hebrews 11:39 AMPC
And all of these, though they won divine approval by means of their faith, did not receive the fulfillment of what was promised.

Ephesians 6:13-14 AMPC
Therefore put on God's complete armor, that you may be able to resist and stand your ground on the evil day of danger, and, having done all the crisis demands, to stand firmly in your place. Stand therefore hold your ground....

Life throws a lot of stuff our way but we must stand in faith. Paul said, "We are troubled on every side, yet not distressed; we are perplexed, but not in despair; Persecuted, but not forsaken; cast down, but not destroyed.... (2 Corinthians 4:8-9).

Faith doesn't always change our reality but it will change us to fit the reality.

We've prayed and cried in faith waiting for the manifestation but don't lose faith while waiting. Continue to stand regardless of the outcome.

Romans 8:38-39
For I am persuaded, that neither death, nor life, nor angels, nor principalities, nor powers, nor things present, nor things to come, Nor height, nor depth, nor any other creature, shall be able to separate us from the love of God, which is in Christ Jesus our Lord.

The heroes of faith went through great trials and tribulations and they landed on their feet because of their faith.

Job lost everything. The Bible says, "Then Job arose, and rent his mantle, and shaved his head, and fell down upon the ground, and worshipped. (Job 1:20).
His faith was challenged. Yes, he mourned but he also worshipped. Out of All the punches the enemy threw at him, Job still landed on his feet.

You too, will land on your feet. Just know, Faith is still Faith through it all.....the good and the bad, ups and downs, riches and poverty, sickness and in health. Stand in your faith.

Habakkuk 2:4
........but the just shall live by his faith.

Romans 1:17
.... The just shall live by faith.

Galatians 3:11
.... for, The just shall live by faith.

Hebrews 10:38
Now the just shall live by faith: ....

The only way to land on our feet, we the JUST must LIVE by FAITH!!!!

HIS WORD

Hebrews 4:12
For the word of God is quick, and powerful, and sharper than any two-edged sword, piercing even to the dividing asunder of soul and spirit, and of the joints and marrow, and is a discerner of the thoughts and intents of the heart.

Psalm 33:4
For the word of the Lord is right; and all his works are done in truth.

Isaiah 53:5
But he was wounded for our transgressions, he was bruised for our iniquities: the chastisement of our peace was upon him; and with his stripes we are healed.

The next time you are tempted to speak the word of the doctor, the loan officer, the enemy, and even the jealous family members...... SPEAK GOD's WORD. His Word can't fail!!!!!

Isaiah 55:11
So shall my word be that goeth forth out of my mouth: it shall not return unto me void, but it shall accomplish that which I please, and it shall prosper in the thing whereto I sent it.

Genesis 1:3,6,9,11,14,20,24,26,29
And God said, Let there be light: and there was light. And God said, Let there be a firmament in the midst of the waters, ... And God said, ... *and it was so.* And God said, ... *and it was so.* And God said, Let there be lights in the firmament of the heaven .... And God said, Let the waters bring forth abundantly .... And God said, Let the earth bring forth the living creature after his kind, ...: *and it was so.* And God said, Let us make man in our image, after our likeness: .... And God said, ...

Speak God's Word and you will experience *AND IT WAS SO* manifestations. His Word is what matters.

OBEDIENCE, A LEARNED BEHAVIOR WHICH YIELDS, THE BLESSING

Romans 5:19
For as by one man's disobedience many were made sinners, so by the obedience of one shall many be made righteous.

Hebrews 5:8 NKJV
though He was a Son, yet He learned obedience by the things which He suffered.

Have the Lord God Almighty given you a word to speak or a task for you to do? Why haven't you obeyed? We've all heard, Obedience is better than sacrifice (1 Samuel 15:22)

There are blessings in obedience.

1 Peter 1:2 AMPC
Who were chosen and foreknown by God the Father and consecrated (sanctified, made holy) by the Spirit to be obedient to Jesus Christ (the Messiah) and to be sprinkled with His blood: May grace (spiritual blessing) and peace be given you in increasing abundance that spiritual peace to be realized in and through Christ, freedom from fears, agitating passions, and moral conflicts.

Genesis 22:16-18 NLT
"This is what the LORD says: Because you have obeyed me and have not withheld even your son, your only son, I swear by my own name that I will certainly bless you. I will multiply your descendants beyond number, like the stars in the sky and the sand on the seashore. Your descendants will conquer the cities of their enemies. And through your descendants all the nations of the earth will be blessed-all because you have obeyed me."

Exodus 20:6 NLT
But I lavish unfailing love for a thousand generations on those who love me and obey my commands.

Deuteronomy 28:1-2 NLT
"If you fully obey the LORD your God and carefully keep all his commands that I am giving you today, the LORD your God will set you high above all the nations of the world. You will experience all these blessings if you obey the LORD your God:

Matthew 8:27 NLT
The disciples were amazed. "Who is this man?" they asked. "Even the winds and waves obey him!"

Do you want to live the blessed life? Obey God.

Blessings are the results of obedience.

No more excuses

Exodus 4:10
And Moses said unto the Lord, O my Lord, I am not eloquent, neither heretofore, nor since thou hast spoken unto thy servant: but I am slow of speech, and of a slow tongue.

Jeremiah 1:6
Then said I, Ah, Lord God! behold, I cannot speak: for I am a child.

Luke 1:18
And Zacharias said unto the angel, Whereby shall I know this? for I am an old man, and my wife well stricken in years.

How many times have God given you an idea, a word to take action on, or told you to step out and do something? But you gave Him an excuse.
God spoke worlds into existence. He created every living thing. All the trees, plants, grass, ponds, rivers, and oceans are His. He created us in His image and breathed His very spirit into us, and we have the audacity to give Him an excuse why we can't do something.

Imagine this, you bake a homemade pound cake. Your grandmother passed down her recipe to you. No one else in the family has the recipe because you are grandma's favorite. Following the recipe step by step, you create a masterpiece that many will enjoy.
Some people want two dips of homemade ice cream to eat with pound cake but not with yours. Your pound cake is so good, people want to enjoy it piece by piece. It's so moist, that it melts in the mouth. Your pound cake is perfectly sweet. It's spongy and soft but yet firm that when it's sliced,

it never crumbles. As it enters the mouths of family and friends it's like a festival going on inside. It's perfect. It put smiles on faces. It makes people think of the good ole days. You didn't add ingredients that wasn't in the recipe. You didn't add grapefruit or nutmeg when it called for water and butter.

The same is true with God. He created masterpieces. Whatever is in His Spirit is in our spirit. EXCUSES is not one of His ingredients.

Exodus 4:11-12
And the Lord said unto him, Who hath made man's mouth? or who maketh the dumb, or deaf, or the seeing, or the blind? have not I the Lord? Now therefore go, and I will be with thy mouth, and teach thee what thou shalt say.

Jeremiah 1:7-9
But the Lord said unto me, Say not, I am a child: for thou shalt go to all that I shall send thee, and whatsoever I command thee thou shalt speak. Be not afraid of their faces: for I am with thee to deliver thee, saith the Lord. Then the Lord put forth his hand, and touched my mouth. And the Lord said unto me, Behold, I have put my words in thy mouth.

Luke 1:19-20
And the angel answering said unto him, I am Gabriel, that stand in the presence of God; and am sent to speak unto thee, and to shew thee these glad tidings. And, behold, thou shalt be dumb, and not able to speak, until the day that these things shall be performed, because thou believest not my words, which shall be fulfilled in their season.

Well, God created YOU.......His masterpiece. He knew what He put in you and how you will impact the lives of those He send you to. Moses stuttered and still led millions through the wilderness. Jeremiah battled with his age, thinking he was too young to be used by God. But he became one of Israel's major prophets. While Zacharias thought he was too old and his wife was barren. But their son led the way for nations to receive Jesus Christ as Lord and Savior.

When we give EX CUSES we miss our divine assignments (cues) in this season where God Holy Spirit will manifest signs, wonders, miracles and that great outpouring of His Spirit during the end time revival.

Our lives are not about us. It's about leading others to Jesus Christ.

Psalm 81:10
I am the Lord thy God, which brought thee out of the land of Egypt: open thy mouth wide, and I will fill it.

Matthew 24:35
Heaven and earth shall pass away, but my words shall not pass away.

God is not changing His mind.
No more excuses. This is the time God wants to use you.
Jesus said, " Verily, verily, I say unto you, He that believeth on me, the works that I do shall he do also; and greater works than these shall he do; because I go unto my Father. (John 14:12 KJV)"

No more excuses

GET READY!!!!!!

Behold, I will do a new thing; now it shall spring forth; shall ye not know it? I will even make a way in the wilderness, and rivers in the desert.   Isaiah 43:19

And I will make them and the places round about my hill a blessing; and I will cause the shower to come down in his season; there shall be showers of blessing.   Ezekiel 34:26

Sometimes LIFE lowers your expectation especially when the same old problems come knocking on the door. But I hear God Almighty saying, "GET READY. I'm bringing you out a different way. I'm blessing you in a new way. GET READY".

I dare you to declare, "I'm raising my expectations. I'm asking BIG. I want every blessing God has for me".

Praise the God and Father of our Lord Jesus Christ! Through Christ, God has blessed us with every spiritual blessing that heaven has to offer.   Ephesians 1:3 GW

In 1 Kings 18 Elijah prayed expecting a mighty move from God. God went beyond Elijah's expectation.

1 Kings 18:41 And Elijah said unto Ahab, Get thee up, eat and drink; for there is a sound of abundance of rain.

Are you ready for God Almighty to show up and show off in your life?

GET READY!!!!

And (Elijah) said to his servant, Go up now, look toward the sea. And he went up, and looked, and said, There is nothing. And he said, Go again seven times. And it came to pass at the seventh time, that he said, Behold, there ariseth a little cloud out of the sea, like a man's hand. And he said, Go up, say unto Ahab, Prepare thy chariot, and get thee down, that the rain stop thee not. 1 Kings 18:43-44

God wants to blow your mind but you must raise your expectation and GET READY.

Ephesians 3:20 AMPC
Now to Him Who, by (in consequence of) the action of His power that is at work within us, is able to carry out His purpose and do superabundantly, far over and above all that we dare ask or think infinitely beyond our highest prayers, desires, thoughts, hopes, or dreams--

It's awesome that we read God's Word. But now it's time to BELIEVE God's Word. We encourage others by telling them, "He never changes. He's always the same".

Well, stand in the mirror and tell yourself. It's time for you to raise your expectation.

I keep hearing, "GET READY".

That thing you've been hoping for, praying about, expecting God to manifest.......raise your expectations and GET READY.

.........no good thing will He withhold from them that walk uprightly. Psalm 84:11

But without faith it is impossible to please him: for he that cometh to God must believe that he is, and that he is a rewarder of them that diligently seek him.   Hebrews 11:6

I urge you to GET READY!!!!!!

LET THIS MIND BE IN YOU

Be mindful of His covenant forever, the promise which He commanded and established to a thousand generations, The covenant which He made with Abraham, and His sworn promise to Isaac.   1 Chronicles 16:15-16 AMPC

Satan desires to side-track us in thinking, we are not important to God Almighty. Or He has better things to think about than us and our problems. But the devil (Satan) is the father of all lies (John 8:44).

The Lord hath been mindful of us: he will bless us; he will bless the house of Israel; he will bless the house of Aaron. He will bless them that fear the Lord, both small and great. The Lord shall increase you more and more, you and your children. Ye are blessed of the Lord which made heaven and earth. Psalm 115:12-15

The Mind of our Heavenly Father should be evident in our mind set. We should start our day by renewing our mind with God's Word.

Thou wilt keep him in perfect peace, whose mind is stayed on thee: because he trusteth in thee. Trust ye in the Lord for ever: for in the Lord Jehovah is everlasting strength: Isaiah 26:3-4

This I recall to my mind, therefore have I hope. It is of the Lord's mercies that we are not consumed, because his compassions fail not. They are new every morning: great is thy faithfulness. Lamentations 3:21-23

Daily renewal of the mind, gives the devil a black eye. He cannot fool us by using trickery in his words.

Why? Because we renew our mind with God's Word. We know what God says about us. We know how God loves us. We know that we are the apple of His eye (Deut 32:10, Psalm 17:8, Lam 2:18, Zechariah 2:8).

I thank God through Jesus Christ our Lord. So then with the mind I myself serve the law of God; .... Romans 7:25

Jesus our Lord and Savior, had the Will of God on His mind and His thoughts overtook Him that God Almighty received all glory out of Jesus' life.

Let this mind be in you, which was also in Christ Jesus: Philippians 2:5

I can of mine own self do nothing: as I hear, I judge: and my judgment is just; because I seek not mine own will, but the will of the Father which hath sent me. John 5:30

For whosoever shall do the will of my Father which is in heaven, the same is my brother, and sister, and mother. Matthew 12:50

And be constantly renewed in the spirit of your mind having a fresh mental and spiritual attitude. Ephesians 4:23 AMPC

Finally, be ye all of one mind, having compassion one of another, love as brethren, be pitiful, be courteous: 1 Peter 3:8

If we allow God Holy Spirit to renew our mind (yes, we must do our part), the enemy can't defeat us because we will have the Mind of Christ. When we think God's thought, we will see the manifold blessings in our lives.

Let this Mind be in you.

AM I TOO LOUD?
GET OVER IT!!!

Psalm 34:1
I will bless the Lord at all times: his praise shall continually be in my mouth.

Psalm 47:1 AMPC
O CLAP your hands, all you peoples! Shout to God with the voice of triumph and songs of joy!

Psalm 124:2
If it had not been the Lord who was on our side, when men rose up against us:

King David had a yet praise. He didn't care who liked it or not. For he wasn't doing this unto man but unto our Lord God.

2 Samuel 6:14,16,20-22
And David danced before the Lord with all his might; and David was girded with a linen ephod. And as the ark of the Lord came into the city of David, Michal Saul's daughter looked through a window, and saw king David leaping and dancing before the Lord; and she despised him in her heart. Then David returned to bless his household. And Michal the daughter of Saul came out to meet David, and said, How glorious was the king of Israel to day, who uncovered himself to day in the eyes of the handmaids of his servants, as one of the vain fellows shamelessly uncovereth himself! And David said unto Michal, It was before the Lord, which chose me before thy father, and before all his house, to appoint me ruler over the people of the Lord, over Israel: therefore will I play before the Lord. And I will yet be more vile than thus, and will be base in mine own sight: and of the maidservants which thou hast spoken of, of them shall I be had in honour.

After all you've been through. Do you have a yet praise?

Are my HALLELUJAHs too loud? Or my THANK YOU JESUS, disturbing you?

Oh well, I will yet be more vile than this, in Praising my God!!!

Acts 16:25-26 AMPC
But about midnight, as Paul and Silas were praying and singing hymns of praise to God, and the other prisoners were listening to them, Suddenly there was a great earthquake, so that the very foundations of the prison were shaken; and at once all the doors were opened and everyone's shackles were unfastened.

Apostle Paul and Silas had to be loud, if the other prisoners heard them. But then there was a great earthquake.

Just imagine, instead of magnifying your problem, you begin to act like King David, Apostle Paul and Silas, you begin to magnify GOD ALMIGHTY. Everything around you, everything that's affected by the problem, and everything that's causing the problem feels the great earthquake of praise. God dispatches legions of Angels to war on your behalf, deliver the answer, and make your enemies bless you abundantly.

But then your haters start complaining you too loud.
So!

Let the redeemed of the Lord say so, whom he hath redeemed from the hand of the enemy (Psalm 107:2); for He is good: for His mercy endureth for ever (Psalm 107:1).

Be encouraged. Do not allow anyone to silence your praise. The Lord God been good to all of us. Keep praying. Keep seeking. Keep praising. Keep worshipping.

Am I too loud? Get over it!!!

To know Him

1 Corinthians 2:2
For I determined not to know any thing among you, save Jesus Christ, and him crucified.

Philippians 3:10 AMPC
For my determined purpose is that I may know Him that I may progressively become more deeply and intimately acquainted with Him, perceiving and recognizing and understanding the wonders of His Person more strongly and more clearly, and that I may in that same way come to know the power outflowing from His resurrection which it exerts over believers, and that I may so share His sufferings as to be continually transformed in spirit into His likeness even to His death, in the hope

Have you ever wondered, "why does Jesus Christ love me so much?".

He loved us so much because of God the Father. "Jesus said to them, My food (nourishment) is to do the will (pleasure) of Him Who sent Me and to accomplish and completely finish His work (John 4:34 AMPC)."
His desire was to please His Father and that meant taking on the sins of the world.

Psalm 78:38
But He, being full of compassion, forgave their iniquity, and destroyed them not: yea, many a time turned he his anger away, and did not stir up all his wrath.

Psalm 145:8
The Lord is gracious, and full of compassion; slow to anger, and of great mercy.

To know Him.

Why did He have suffered abuse, disrespect, pain, and rejection for us?

Isaiah 53:3-5
He is despised and rejected of men; a man of sorrows, and acquainted with grief: and we hid as it were our faces from him; he was despised, and we esteemed him not. Surely he hath borne our griefs, and carried our sorrows: yet we did esteem him stricken, smitten of God, and afflicted. But he was wounded for our transgressions, he was bruised for our iniquities: the chastisement of our peace was upon him; and with his stripes we are healed.

Jesus love us beyond Himself. He did all of this so we wouldn't have too.
He took the beatings. He took the spitting. He took the cursing. He took sickness and disease. He took poverty. He took what should've been ours because He love us so.

To know Him.

What kind of love is this?

John 15:13
Greater love hath no man than this, that a man lay down his life for his friends.

Desire to know Him, and He will reveal Himself to you.

To know Him is my desire.

GREAT IS HIS FAITHFULNESS

John 3:16
For God so loved the world, that he gave his only begotten
Son, that whosoever believeth in him should not perish, but
have everlasting life.

Have you ever considered how faithful God is to you? Even
when you're not faithful, He's still faithful.

Psalm 89:1 AMPC
I WILL sing of the mercy and loving-kindness of the Lord
forever; with my mouth will I make known Your faithfulness
from generation to generation.

Isaiah 25:1 AMPC
O LORD, You are my God; I will exalt You, I will praise Your
name, for You have done wonderful things, even purposes
planned of old and fulfilled in faithfulness and truth.

Lamentations 3:21-23 AMPC
But this I recall and therefore have I hope and expectation: It
is because of the Lord's mercy and loving-kindness that we are
not consumed, because His tender compassions fail not. They
are new every morning; great and abundant is Your stability
and faithfulness.

The Bible defines faithful as, loyal, firm, not changing,
steadfast, constant, unwavering, dedicated, and committed.

We can all agree, these are some of the attributes to describe
our Father God.

When we were yet sinners, doing our own thing.......God Almighty committed His love and Devotion to us. Since we've became believers we haven't always been faithful in our giving...... in what God Holy Spirit put in our heart to give, speaking...... what He tells us to speak, operating in the spiritual gifts when He tells us to, or praying when He says pray, and yet He's still Faithful.

1 Corinthians 1:9
God is faithful, by whom ye were called unto the fellowship of his Son Jesus Christ our Lord.

1 Thessalonians 5:24
Faithful is he that calleth you, who also will do it.

Thank God, HE is nothing like man.
God doesn't cancel His plan for our lives just because we're acting crazy or out of sync with Him. He still loves us. His compassion is still towards us. He's still faithful to His Word and us. He is faithful!!!

2 Thessalonians 3:3 AMPC
Yet the Lord is faithful, and He will strengthen you and set you on a firm foundation and guard you from the evil one.

Father God, in Jesus Christ teach me how to be faithful to you. This goes beyond going to church faithfully. I want to be faithfully committed in relationship and intimacy with You. Thank you for Your Commitment, Compassion, Love, and most of all Your Faithfulness to me and my Seed. I believe. I receive. And it is so. In Jesus Christ, Amen.

DO NOT FAINT

And let us not be weary in well doing: for in due season we shall reap, if we faint not. Galatians 6:9

Have God Almighty made you a promise and you are waiting on the manifestation?

Do not give up. Do not give in. Do not faint.

Everything He promised, will come to pass.

For when God made promise to Abraham, because he could swear by no greater, he sware by himself, Saying, Surely blessing I will bless thee, and multiplying I will multiply thee. And so, after he (Abraham) had patiently endured, he obtained the promise. Hebrews 6:13-15

The Lord is not slack concerning his promise, ...2 Peter 3:9

But as it is written, Eye hath not seen, nor ear heard, neither have entered into the heart of man, the things which God hath prepared for them that love him.
1 Corinthians 2:9

When you sow a seed into the ground, it doesn't spring up an hour later. But you water it and cultivate the soil. When you bought the packet of seed, the picture had a beautiful manicured healthy flower but when you opened the packet you found only seeds. On back of the packet it gives instructions how to plant, feed, and when to exposure it to sunlight. Some packets give you the life cycle and what you should be seeing.

The same is true with the promises of God Almighty. God has given us promises. But have you read the instructions? Plant the seed of faith. Make sure you use rich soil which is the Word of the Living God. Water it with praise. Expose it to worship. Repeat a couple of times a week.

So shall My word be that goes forth out of My mouth: it shall not return to Me void without producing any effect, useless, but it shall accomplish that which I please and purpose, and it shall prosper in the thing for which I sent it. Isaiah 55:11 AMPC

For I am the Lord; I will speak, and the word that I shall speak shall be performed (come to pass); it shall be no more delayed or prolonged, for in your days, ..., I will speak the word and will perform it, says the Lord God. Ezekiel 12:25 AMPC

For since the beginning of the world men have not heard, nor perceived by the ear, neither hath the eye seen, O God, beside thee, what he hath prepared for him that waiteth for him. Isaiah 64:4

For all the promises of God in him are yea, and in him Amen, unto the glory of God by us.
2 Corinthians 1:20

Do not faint. The promise is on the way.

HE IS

Isaiah 9:6
For unto us a child is born, unto us a son is given: and the
government shall be upon his shoulder: and his name shall be
called Wonderful, Counsellor, The mighty God, The
everlasting Father, The Prince of Peace.

Revelation 22:13
I am Alpha and Omega, the beginning and the end, the first
and the last.

Genesis 17:1
..........I am the Almighty God; ......

Exodus 3:14
.........I AM THAT I AM: ....

Psalm 81:10
I am the Lord thy God, which brought thee out of the land of
Egypt: open thy mouth wide, and I will fill it.

Matthew 28:20
..............I am with you always, even unto the end of the
world....

Now that we know who Jesus is, let's declare to the heavens:

Blessed be the Name of the Living God.
Almighty He is.
Wonderful He is.
Awesome He is
His works are Excellent.
He gives unto me His Love.
His Peace blankets me.
And He Restores me, second by second of every minute.

TGIF
THANK GOD I'M FREE

John 8:36
If the Son therefore shall make you free, ye shall be free indeed.

What is the definition of FREE?

The bible says, one that is not bound.

Our pocket says, no charge or zero cost.

Romans 6:18
Being then made free from sin, ye became the servants of righteousness.

Romans 6:22
But now being made free from sin, and become servants to God, ye have your fruit unto holiness, and the end everlasting life.

Being free cost Jesus Christ His life and we are no longer slaves to sin. Hallelujah.

So now we do those things that promote Holiness which leads us to everlasting life with our Lord and Savior.

Romans 8:2 AMPC
For the law of the Spirit of life which is in Christ Jesus the law of our new being has freed me from the law of sin and of death.

We are free from sickness and disease. We are free from poverty and lack. We are free from burdens and strongholds.

Jesus said in Luke 4:18 NLT

"The Spirit of the LORD is upon me, for he has anointed me to bring Good News to the poor. He has sent me to proclaim that captives will be released, that the blind will see, that the oppressed will be set free, and that the time of the LORD's favor has come."

Psalm 34:4 NLT
I prayed to the LORD, and He answered me. He freed me from all my fears.

TGIF
Thank God I'm FREE

THROUGH IT ALL.......

Romans 10:17
So then faith cometh by hearing, and hearing by the word of God.

Jeremiah 29:11
For I know the thoughts that I think toward you, saith the Lord, thoughts of peace, and not of evil, to give you an expected end.

Sometimes we become anxious for our present life to catch up to our future. But I'm so glad God Almighty never gives up on us. We wishfully think of stuff for our lives instead of seeking Father God for His plan for us. But through it all, He's still there for us, waiting for us to ask for His assistance.

Ephesians 1:3 NLT
All praise to God, the Father of our Lord Jesus Christ, who has blessed us with every spiritual blessing in the heavenly realms because we are united with Christ.

Galatians 3:29 NLT
And now that you belong to Christ, you are the true children of Abraham. You are his heirs, and God's promise to Abraham belongs to you.

Psalm 119:116-117 NLT
LORD, sustain me as you promised, that I may live! Do not let my hope be crushed. Sustain me, and I will be rescued; then I will meditate continually on your decrees.

No matter what's going on in your life, God want to help. He wants you to know, "I'm here for you my child".

Psalm 23:1
The Lord is my shepherd; I shall not want.

There's no need to fear, you will not lack, be without, or live in poverty.

Psalm 23:3
He restoreth my soul: he leadeth me in the paths of righteousness for his name's sake.
I renew you with my strength and make you whole. I show you what is right and what will bring Me Glory.

Psalm 23:4
Yea, though I walk through the valley of the shadow of death, I will fear no evil: for thou art with me; thy rod and thy staff they comfort me.

As you walk through this dark, evil and deadly world, do not be alarmed, frightened, or stressed, I am with you always, even unto the ends of the world. I AM close to you. I am the Good Shepherd, My rod and staff protects and comforts you.

Through it all, our Lord and Savior is still with us. God is committed to you because He want to be. Through all the tests and trials, doubts and fears, THE MOST HIGH GOD, is with you.

Find in Him your resting place.... peace and tranquility is there, love and wholeness is there, healing and good health is there, deliverance is there.

2 Corinthians 3:17
Now the Lord is that Spirit: and where the Spirit of the Lord is, there is liberty.

Through it all............

NOTHING CAN STOP GOD'S PLAN FOR YOUR LIFE

Ephesians 1:3 NLT
All praise to God, the Father of our Lord Jesus Christ, who has blessed us with every spiritual blessing in the heavenly realms because we are united with Christ.

Nothing takes God Almighty by surprise. He's all knowing.

Exodus 1:15-16,22
And the king of Egypt spake to the Hebrew midwives, of which the name of the one was Shiphrah, and the name of the other Puah: And he said, When ye do the office of a midwife to the Hebrew women, and see them upon the stools; if it be a son, then ye shall kill him: but if it be a daughter, then she shall live. And Pharaoh charged all his people, saying, Every son that is born ye shall cast into the river, and every daughter ye shall save alive.

When God has a plan for you, NOTHING can stop it!

Jeremiah 29:11 AMPC
For I know the thoughts and plans that I have for you, says the Lord, thoughts and plans for welfare and peace and not for evil, to give you hope in your final outcome.

Matthew 2:13,16
And when they were departed, behold, the angel of the Lord appeareth to Joseph in a dream, saying, Arise, and take the young child and his mother, and flee into Egypt, and be thou there until I bring thee word: for Herod will seek the young child to destroy him. Then Herod, when he saw that he was mocked of the wise men, was exceeding wroth, and sent forth, and slew all the children that were in Bethlehem, and in all the coasts thereof, from two years old and under, according to the time which he had diligently enquired of the wise men.

Satan has plotted against us but the last promise Jesus Christ made to us was:
"Behold, I give unto you power to tread on serpents and scorpions, and over all the power of the enemy: and nothing shall by any means hurt you" (Luke 10:19).

Isaiah 54:17 NLT
But in that coming day no weapon formed against you will succeed. You will silence every voice raised up to accuse you. These benefits are enjoyed by the servants of the LORD; their vindication will come from me. I, the LORD, have spoken!

We should know by now, whatever GOD MOST HIGH, speaks, it will come to pass.

Satan plotted against Moses and Jesus, but instead, there were miscarriages in the incubators of every satanic and evil womb. Nothing can penetrate the perimeters of God's Word.

Hebrews 4:12
For the word of God is quick, and powerful, and sharper than any twoedged sword, piercing even to the dividing asunder of soul and spirit, and of the joints and marrow, and is a discerner of the thoughts and intents of the heart.

Whatever God promises, His Word is POWERFUL and it backs up every promise. What a Mighty God we serve!

Moses had a mighty call on his life, to deliver God's people. And you know, Our Savior and Lord Jesus Christ came to deliver us. Hallelujah
The enemy can't destroy Gods Plan!

By the authority of Christ Jesus, I bind every blocking and hindering spirit that's delaying the manifestation of blessing upon your life. In Jesus Christ. Amen.

Some of us are in labor in the spirit realm, and I stand in the gap as the midwife.
And I say, BREATHE!!!
Now PUSH.
YOU CAN'T GIVE UP NOW!!!
You WILL NOT miscarry!!
Take a rest.
Now Breathe and push.
Pray until something happens

Nothing can stop God's Plan for your life

Now rejoice in the God of your salvation.

Rejoice in the Lord always: and again I say, Rejoice.
Philippians 4:4

FAITH GIVES YOU RIGHTS

Matthew 17:20
And Jesus said unto them, …….. for verily I say unto you, If ye have faith as a grain of mustard seed, ye shall say unto this mountain, Remove hence to yonder place; and it shall remove; and nothing shall be impossible unto you.

Jesus always operated in FAITH. When He spoke change happened.

The late Bishop L. E. Willis, Sr. coined a phrase, "Faith in God spends like money with the merchant."

In Every Kingdom there are Kings and there are rights. In America we have the Bill of Rights and laws. The Only way for them to work for you, is that you must know your rights.

In 2 Kings 4:14-20, This woman received a prophetic word from Elisha the Prophet. He prophesied to her a son. Her faith was ignited by what she heard with her ears.

So then faith cometh by hearing, and hearing by the word of God. Romans 10:17

That season arrived and this woman had a son. Well, when the boy was a little older he died on his mother's lap. The Bible says, "And she went up, and laid him on the bed of the man of God, and shut the door upon him, and went out. And she called unto her husband, and said, Send me, I pray thee, one of the young men, and one of the asses, that I may run to the man of God, and come again (2 Kings 4:21-22)."

She went to where the prophet was. Speaking FAITH, this woman had already pronounced, "ALL IS WELL". She knew God was able to do anything!!! She went to the one God spoke through. Her faith was in action, so much so, that she got the attention of Prophet Elisha, without her screaming, yelling, and falling out.

When you know you have rights, you don't have to get emotional.

In our society if a driver runs a red light and hit you while you proceeding through the green light, that driver is at fault. When you go to court, the judge only wants to hear the facts. This driver hit me even though I had the RIGHT of way. The judge will find that driver guilty and he must pay you for all damages. Why? Because you had faith in your legal system and you knew your rights.

Well this is true with us. Our legal system is GOD's Kingdom, our judge is God almighty, and our attorney is Christ Jesus.

This woman knew her rights. Her faith is in God's legal system. The Bible says in 2 Kings 4:32-35, Elisha went to her house and went into the room where the boy laid dead. Elisha prayed and then he laid on the child, and the child's body was warm. Elisha got up, went out and walked around. Then he went back into the room and laid on the child again. The child sneezed seven times and then opened his eyes.

The woman didn't have to beg nor cry, she believed. Her faith determined her outcome.

Do you have situations in your life that was the result of the manifested Word of God?

Do not beg God. Do not cry.

The Bible says this four times, "The JUST shall live by FAITH" (Hab 2:4, Rom 1:17, Gal 3:11, and Heb 10:38).

LIVE BY FAITH!!!

We must know our rights as citizens of God's Kingdom.

If you sick, in pain, or depressed, know your rights. Isaiah 53:5 By His (JESUS) stripes we are healed.

We don't have to ask for this. It's our right as a citizen of God's Kingdom.

Do you have more bills than money?
You have rights. Philippians 4:19 But my God shall supply all your need according to his riches in glory by Christ Jesus.

Are your children off track?
Proverbs 11:21 ....but the seed of the righteous shall be delivered.
Psalm 112:1-2 Praise the LORD! Blessed is the man who fears the LORD, Who delights greatly in His commandments. His descendants will be mighty on earth; The generation of the upright will be blessed.

Live by FAITH so you can enjoy your rights as a citizen.

I decree I'll never be sick because I have a right to live in good health. I'll never be broke because I have the right of having ALL my need supplied by God. My children are delivered, saved, and filled with God Holy Spirit. They will be successful in the pulpit and the boardroom. They will be mighty on this earth because I will remind the high court of my rights as a citizen.

Faith cometh by hearing and hearing by the Word of God.
It's time to know your rights in God's Kingdom.

Faith gives you rights

REJOICE!! REJOICE!!!

This is the day which the Lord hath made; we will rejoice and be glad in it. Psalm 118:24

Rejoice in the Lord, O ye righteous: for praise is comely for the upright. For our heart shall rejoice in him, because we have trusted in his holy name. Psalm 33:1, 21

As you go about your day, rejoice in the God of your strength. Life will throw everything at you but you, rejoice in the Most High God.

For there is a reward in rejoicing:
Thou wilt keep him in perfect peace, whose mind is stayed on thee: because he trusteth in thee. Isaiah 26:3

I rejoice in your word like one who discovers a great treasure. I will praise you seven times a day because all your regulations are just. Psalm 119:162,164 NLT

.... for this day is holy to our Lord. And be not grieved and depressed, for the joy of the Lord is your strength and stronghold. Nehemiah 8:10 AMPC

REJOICE!!! REJOICE!!!!

Don't rejoice because you feel good but rejoice because HE IS GOOD.

Don't rejoice because of your job promotion but rejoice because the LORD is your salvation, shield and buckler, strong tower, healer, way maker, provider, Providence, sustainer, deliverer, Saviour, your Great Emancipator, and covenant keeping God.

REJOICE!!! REJOICE!!!

And again I say REJOICE!!!!

STAND ON THE PROMISE

Have you received everything God promised you?

Psalm 105:42
For he remembered his holy promise, and Abraham his servant.

Many of us have not seen the manifestation of every promise God made to us but we must STAND on the promise.

Isaiah 49:31 MSG
But those who wait upon God get fresh strength. They spread their wings and soar like eagles, They run and don't get tired, they walk and don't lag behind.

One of many things we can attest to, is that God can't lie.

Romans 4:13,16
For the promise, that he should be the heir of the world, was not to Abraham, or to his seed, through the law, but through the righteousness of faith. Therefore it is of faith, that it might be by grace; to the end the promise might be sure to all the seed; not to that only which is of the law, but to that also which is of the faith of Abraham; who is the father of us all,

We are the seed of Abraham and we must stand in hope waiting on the promise. Standing in hope is not standing still and expecting God to do everything. But we stand, still moving in that God has called us to while waiting on the promise.

We occupy ourselves till the promise come.

Abraham received the promise by faith in his spirit and kept growing in his intimacy with God.

Romans 4:17-21
(As it is written, I have made thee a father of many nations,) before him whom he believed, even God, who quickeneth the dead, and calleth those things which be not as though they were. Who against hope believed in hope, that he might become the father of many nations; according to that which was spoken, So shall thy seed be. And being not weak in faith, he considered not his own body now dead, when he was about an hundred years old, neither yet the deadness of Sara's womb: He staggered not at the promise of God through unbelief; but was strong in faith, giving glory to God; And being fully persuaded that, what he had promised, he was able also to perform.

People will tell you to give up because they don't see it happening, but I encourage you don't go by what you see.

Just know, God is able to do superabundantly far over and above all that we [dare] ask or think [infinitely beyond our highest prayers, desires, thoughts, hopes, or dreams]— Ephesians 3:20 AMPC.

Isaiah 55:11 AMPC
So shall My word be that goes forth out of My mouth: it shall not return to Me void without producing any effect, useless, but it shall accomplish that which I please and purpose, and it shall prosper in the thing for which I sent it.

I leave you with a scripture that stimulated me when doubt tried to overtake me:

Psalm 119:49-50 AMPC
Lord God, Remember fervently the word and promise to Your servant, in which You have caused me to hope. This is my comfort and consolation in my affliction: that Your word has revived me and given me life.

PRAYERS OF THE RIGHTEOUS

...............The earnest prayer of a righteous person has great power and produces wonderful results. James 5:16 NLT

The enemy tries to deceive us by telling us, "God is not listening" but Satan is a liar.

Psalm 17:6 AMPC
I have called upon You, O God, for You will hear me; incline Your ear to me and hear my speech.

Psalm 40:1 AMPC
I WAITED patiently and expectantly for the Lord; and He inclined to me and heard my cry.

I get excited in knowing the Lord God gets excited when we call to Him.

Jeremiah 33:3
Call unto me, and I will answer thee, and shew thee great and mighty things, which thou knowest not.

This is what Hannah did, she made her request known unto God.

1 Samuel 1:10-13
And she was in bitterness of soul, and prayed unto the Lord, and wept sore. And she vowed a vow, and said, O Lord of hosts, if thou wilt indeed look on the affliction of thine handmaid, and remember me, and not forget thine handmaid, but wilt give unto thine handmaid a man child, then I will give him unto the Lord all the days of his life, and there shall no razor come upon his head. And it came to pass, as she continued praying before the Lord, that Eli marked her mouth. Now Hannah, she spake in her heart; only her lips moved, but her voice was not heard: ....

God Almighty heard the prayer of Hannah, and Samuel was the answer manifested.

I've learned whatever concerns us, concerns God. Every detail of our life concerns God. He want us to trust Him by making our request known unto Him.

1 John 5:14-15
And this is the confidence that we have in him, that, if we ask any thing according to his will, he heareth us: And if we know that he hear us, whatsoever we ask, we know that we have the petitions that we desired of him.

Do you have a situation that need God's intervention?

I dare you to pray and call unto our Lord God Yeshua. Watch Him show up and show out. He did it for Peter.

Acts 12:5,12-13
Peter therefore was kept in prison: but prayer was made without ceasing of the church unto God for him. And when he had considered the thing, he came to the house of Mary the mother of John, whose surname was Mark; where many were gathered together praying. And as Peter knocked at the door of the gate, a damsel came to hearken, named Rhoda.

There was a prayer meeting going on. The high court threw Peter in jail, but the saints prayed to the high courts of Heaven and God Most High sent His angels. The angels released Peter. Hallelujah. God is so awesome.

Our Sovereign God heard the prayers of the righteous and He responded. It's something great when the righteous is on one accord. Healing takes place. Deliverance takes place. Freedom takes place.

Hannah prayed asking God for a son and God immediately answered her. Peter was locked in jail for preaching the Gospel, but the saints were praying and God sent His angels. While the prayer meeting was still going on, the Angels of the Lord God released Peter and he went to where the prayer meeting was. What a mighty God we serve.

In 1980, Dr Charles G. Hayes and the Cosmopolitan Church released a song, "JESUS CAN WORK IT OUT". Some of the lyrics in that song says, "While you trying to figure it out. God has already worked it out".

Imagine this.......
You having a situation and you reach out to some of the saints and we're on one accord but while we praying, God Almighty send His angels to deliver and manifest the answer.

What would you do?

Psalm 34:15,17
The eyes of the Lord are upon the righteous, and his ears are open unto their cry. The righteous cry, and the Lord heareth, and delivereth them out of all their troubles.

The effectual fervent prayer of a righteous man availeth much. James 5:16

WHAT ARE YOU THINKING ABOUT?

Proverbs 23:7 NKJV
For as he thinks in his heart, so is he. ....

Many times our thoughts fast forward into a scary, negative, and accident filled movie. But did you know you can control your thinking?

Apostle Paul admonishes us in
Philippians 4:8-9
Finally, brethren, whatsoever things are true, whatsoever things are honest, whatsoever things are just, whatsoever things are pure, whatsoever things are lovely, whatsoever things are of good report; if there be any virtue, and if there be any praise, think on these things. Those things, which ye have both learned, and received, and heard, and seen in me, do: and the God of peace shall be with you.

When we think back from where God has brought us from, we should be singing HALLELUJAH, all day long.

In Acts 26:2, Apostle Paul said, "I think myself happy".
We must learn to think happy thoughts. Step out your box and think positive thoughts. Change your mind how you see yourself and others. Become an out-of-the-box-thinker.
God promises to keep those in perfect peace whose minds are on Him (Isaiah 26:3).

1 Corinthians 2:16
For who hath known the mind of the Lord, that he may instruct him? But we have the mind of Christ.

Saturate your mind (thinking) with God's Word. Only great things will come of that.

We become what we think. If you think you're not good enough, then you're not.
If you think you are blessed and highly favored, then you are.

Thoughts are so powerful, that the Woman with the issue of blood didn't give in to all those doctor's negative reports. But she thought within herself she was going to get well.

Matthew 9:20-22
And, behold, a woman, which was diseased with an issue of blood twelve years, came behind him, and touched the hem of his garment: For she said within herself, If I may but touch his garment, I shall be whole. But Jesus turned him about, and when he saw her, he said, Daughter, be of good comfort; thy faith hath made thee whole. And the woman was made whole from that hour.

Proverbs 23:7
For as he thinketh in his heart, so is he: ....

RAISE YOUR PRAISE

Psalm 113:3
From the rising of the sun unto the going down of the same the Lord's name is to be praised.

This day is not promised to no man but by His Grace and Mercy we are here.

Psalm 33:1
Rejoice in the Lord, O ye righteous: for praise is comely for the upright.

Psalm 3:3
But thou, O Lord, art a shield for me; my glory, and the lifter up of mine head.

Psalm 44:8
In God we boast all the day long, and praise thy name for ever. Selah.

Let today be different. Instead of complaining, Praise the Lord. Instead of getting upset, Praise the Lord.

Isaiah 12:4
And in that day shall ye say, Praise the Lord, call upon his name, declare his doings among the people, make mention that his name is exalted.

Instead of thinking about what you don't have, PRAISE THE LORD.

Jeremiah 17:14
Heal me, O Lord, and I shall be healed; save me, and I shall be saved: for thou art my praise.

Praise the Lord God because He is good.

Revelation 19:5

And a voice came out of the throne, saying, Praise our God, all ye his servants, and ye that fear him, both small and great.

Let's join in with Heaven's Army, PRAISE YE THE LORD.

1 Peter 2:9
But ye are a chosen generation, a royal priesthood, an holy nation, a peculiar people; that ye should shew forth the praises of him who hath called you out of darkness into his marvellous light:

Raise your praise

CAN YOU IMAGINE

Living a debt free lifestyle
Free from sickness and disease
Having a marriage made in Heaven.
Your household saved and serving the Lord.
ALL your need supplied.

When you raise your desire and expectation for God's Word,
and command your life to line up with what God says......
manifestation happens.

Matthew 6:33 NLT
Seek the Kingdom of God above all else, and live righteously,
and he will give you everything you need.

Psalm 37:4
Delight thyself also in the Lord; and he shall give thee the
desires of thine heart.

Proverbs 10:22
The blessing of the Lord, it maketh rich, and he addeth no
sorrow with it.

Proverbs 18:22 NLT
The man who finds a wife finds a treasure, and he receives
favor from the LORD.

Romans 13:8
Owe no man any thing, but to love one another: ....

Philippians 4:19
But my God shall supply all your need according to his riches
in glory by Christ Jesus.

Psalm 107:20 NLT
He sent out his word and healed them, snatching them from
the door of death.

Joshua 24:15
.... but as for me and my house, we will serve the Lord.

Isaiah 44:3-5 NLT
For I will pour out water to quench your thirst and to irrigate
your parched fields. And I will pour out my Spirit on your
descendants, and my blessing on your children. They will
thrive like watered grass, like willows on a riverbank. Some
will proudly claim, 'I belong to the LORD.' Others will say, 'I
am a descendant of Jacob.' Some will write the LORD's name
on their hands and will take the name of Israel as their own."

Deuteronomy 8:18 GW
But remember the LORD your God is the one who makes you
wealthy. He's confirming the promise which he swore to your
ancestors. It's still in effect today.

Psalm 112:1-3 GW
Hallelujah! Blessed is the person who fears the LORD and is
happy to obey his commands. His descendants will grow
strong on the earth. The family of a decent person will be
blessed. Wealth and riches will be in his home. His
righteousness continues forever.

Psalm 115:14-15
The Lord shall increase you more and more, you and your
children. Ye are blessed of the Lord which made heaven and
earth.

Ecclesiastes 7:11-12 MSG
Wisdom is better when it's paired with money, Especially if
you get both while you're still living. Double protection:
wisdom and wealth! Plus this bonus: Wisdom energizes its
owner.

Imagine that. God want to bless you beyond your wildest
dreams and bring you into the land of more than enough.

HOW BAD DO YOU WANT IT?

Mark 5:25
And a certain woman, which had an issue of blood twelve years,

This woman had to live outside the city because of the laws set forth in Leviticus chapters 12 and 15. She was unclean and she had to wear a bell around her ankle or waist. When she went anywhere outside of her camp she had to announce while ringing the bell, "UNCLEAN. UNCLEAN. UNCLEAN". Which told everyone she was unclean.

Can you imagine in this day and time, if those that have any type of sickness and disease, being put out the city because they are unclean?

This woman couldn't live with her family nor spend any quality time with them. Why? Because she was unclean.

The Bible says in Mark 5:26, "And had suffered many things of many physicians, and had spent all that she had, and was nothing bettered, but rather grew worse,".

Every doctor she went to, took her money and then gave her a bad report. But she kept believing she was going to get better.

Many times, Satan will fight us for the promise God made to us. But we must stand upon His Word.
Jesus said in John 10:10, "I am come that they might have life, and that they might have it more abundantly."
Satan do not want us to be free, whole, healed, delivered, blessed, favored, or filled with abundance.

But we must be like this woman, and encourage ourselves in the Lord.

Talk to yourself and say- I will make it. I am more than a conqueror. I am healed. I am the righteousness of God through Christ Jesus. I am the head. I am the lender. I am above. I am whole. I am the righteous rich. I am more than able.

But then she heard something.
Mark 5:27 says, "When she had heard of Jesus".

What have you heard, lately?

Romans 10:17
So then faith cometh by hearing, and hearing by the word of God.

Mark 5:27-28
When she had heard of Jesus, came in the press behind, and touched his garment. For she said, If I may touch but his clothes, I shall be whole.

What would happen in your life if you stretch your faith like she did?

How bad do you want it?

This woman received her healing miracle because she refused to accept sickness and disease. But she heard of Jesus and her faith led her to her miracle.

Mark 5:29-30,34
And straightway the fountain of her blood was dried up; and she felt in her body that she was healed of that plague. And Jesus, immediately knowing in himself that virtue had gone out of him, turned him about in the press, and said, Who touched my clothes? And he said unto her, Daughter, thy faith hath made thee whole; go in peace, and be whole of thy plague.

Do you want it bad enough to stretch your faith to the unseen realm and snatch your healing, financial increase, deliverance, or salvation for your family?

Pastor Bill Winston said, "Faith determined the outcome before the fight ever started".

Saints of the Most High God, use your faith and believe God for everything you need and want.

How bad do you want it?

YOU ARE CHOSEN

1 Peter 2:9-10
But ye are a chosen generation, a royal priesthood, an holy nation, a peculiar people; that ye should shew forth the praises of him who hath called you out of darkness into his marvellous light: Which in time past were not a people, but are now the people of God: which had not obtained mercy, but now have obtained mercy.

The Creator of the universe chose you to represent Him in this earth. The Master and King, chose you to be His son or daughter. The Most High God chose you.

Ephesians 1:4 NLT
Even before he made the world, God loved us and chose us in Christ to be holy and without fault in his eyes.

You were hand-picked by the King of kings and the Lord of lords. You are the child of the Most High King.

John 15:16
Ye have not chosen me, but I have chosen you, and ordained you, that ye should go and bring forth fruit, and that your fruit should remain: that whatsoever ye shall ask of the Father in my name, he may give it you.

You are a King's Kid. You didn't stand in a line while teams were picked. But our Lord God Almighty had you on His mind and chose you before He laid the foundations of the world.

Now stand up. Put your shoulders back. And walk like Royalty. Know that you were chosen.
Give God glory, honor, and praise for choosing you.

Hallelujah

You are chosen

SPEAK LIFE

Proverbs 18:21 AMPC
Death and life are in the power of the tongue, and they who indulge in it shall eat the fruit of it for death or life.

What is your tongue releasing?

Are you listening to what you're saying?

James 3:5-8
Even so the tongue is a little member, and boasteth great things. Behold, how great a matter a little fire kindleth! And the tongue is a fire, a world of iniquity: so is the tongue among our members, that it defileth the whole body, and setteth on fire the course of nature; and it is set on fire of hell. For every kind of beasts, and of birds, and of serpents, and of things in the sea, is tamed, and hath been tamed of mankind: But the tongue can no man tame; it is an unruly evil, full of deadly poison.

Many times saints blame the devil for what's going wrong in their lives. But maybe they need to consider what they are speaking into the atmosphere.

Years ago I went through much pain and had no one to vent to. So I vented to the Lord in prayer. After I got up I heard the voice of the Lord so clearly. "My daughter, you are speaking death. There's power in words. Put pressure on your mouth. Speak with intent. Speak life and you will see life". His Words changed my life. And it will change yours too, if you allow it.

I quickly put in to Practice everything God told me and I experienced changes immediately. You too can speak life to whatever is going on in your life.

I'm reminded of Christ Jesus. Everywhere He went, He spoke life. But there was one time He spoke death in Matthew 21:18-19

Now in the morning as he returned into the city, he hungered. And when he saw a fig tree in the way, he came to it, and found nothing thereon, but leaves only, and said unto it, Let no fruit grow on thee henceforward for ever. And presently the fig tree withered away.

The fig tree did not produce so Jesus spoke death upon it.

You too have this power. Be careful what you speak for it will happen.

Deuteronomy 30:15,19
See, I have set before thee this day life and good, and death and evil; I call heaven and earth to record this day against you, that I have set before you life and death, blessing and cursing: therefore choose life, that both thou and thy seed may live:

The choice is yours.

Speak Life

YOU HAVE MY WORD

Isaiah 40:8
The grass withereth, the flower fadeth: but the word of our
God shall stand for ever.

Proverbs 4:20-22
My son, attend to my words; incline thine ear unto my sayings.
Let them not depart from thine eyes; keep them in the midst of
thine heart. For they are life unto those that find them, and
health to all their flesh.

Isaiah 55:11
So shall my word be that goeth forth out of my mouth: it shall
not return unto me void, but it shall accomplish that which I
please, and it shall prosper in the thing whereto I sent it.

Matthew 24:35
Heaven and earth shall pass away, but my words shall not pass
away.

John 15:7
If ye abide in me, and my words abide in you, ye shall ask what
ye will, and it shall be done unto you.

1 John 5:14-15
And this is the confidence that we have in him, that, if we ask
any thing according to his will, he heareth us: And if we know
that he hear us, whatsoever we ask, we know that we have the
petitions that we desired of him.

God's Word speaks for Itself.

God's Word won't fail. It will work if you use it.

Selah.

THE POWER OF PRAISE

Psalm 150:6 NKJV
Let everything that has breath praise the LORD. Praise the
LORD!

2 Chronicles 20:3-6,12 NKJV
And Jehoshaphat feared, and set himself to seek the LORD,
and proclaimed a fast throughout all Judah. So Judah
gathered together to ask help from the LORD; and from all the
cities of Judah they came to seek the LORD. Then
Jehoshaphat stood in the assembly of Judah and Jerusalem, in
the house of the LORD, before the new court, and said: "O
LORD God of our fathers, are You not God in heaven, and do
You not rule over all the kingdoms of the nations, and in Your
hand is there not power and might, so that no one is able to
withstand You? O our God, will You not judge them? For we
have no power against this great multitude that is coming
against us; nor do we know what to do, but our eyes are upon
You."

David said in Psalm 141:8, "But my eyes are upon You, O GOD
the Lord; In You I take refuge; Do not leave my soul destitute.
Don't let them kill me".

Let's wake up Apostle Paul and Silas in Acts 16.
They were stripped and beaten, and thrown into prison with
stocks on their feet. But at midnight. Some of us reading this
devotional are experiencing midnight right now in our lives.
But these Apostles, instead of sleeping or having a pity party,
they were praying and singing hymns to God. They had a
praise party. The other prisoners were listening and watching.
You know how the world do it. They want to see how the
saints going to react to unjust treatment. But Paul and Silas
was so sincere with their praise, the Bible says in Acts 16:26,
"Suddenly there was a great earthquake, so that the
foundations of the prison were shaken; and immediately all
the doors were opened and everyone's chains were loose".
Everyone's chains were loosed, not just Paul and Silas.

The power of praise coming from you will not only free you from bondage but it would free those around you: your family, your coworkers, other believers, and even those that been laughing in your face. There is power in praise. Jehoshaphat knew he couldn't win the battle. He was totally surrounded by the enemy on all sides but He knew who had all the power. So he praised his way through to victory.

Praise. Praise. Praise. Praise is comely for the righteous. Raise your praise and watch freedom overtake you.

The Power of Praise

It's the Heart of the Matter

1 Chronicles 17:2
Then Nathan said unto David, Do all that is in thine heart; for God is with thee.

When was your last Heart check-up?

Psalm 51:10
Create in me a clean heart, O God; and renew a right spirit within me.

During an annual physical, the heart is checked using a (EKG) test. This test measures your heart's electrical activity, from how fast the heart beats to how well its chambers conduct electrical energy. But there's a different and more powerful heart test that we need and it's only given by God Holy Spirit.

James 4:8
Draw nigh to God, and he will draw nigh to you. Cleanse your hands, ye sinners; and purify your hearts, ye double minded.

Deuteronomy 30:6
And the Lord thy God will circumcise thine heart, and the heart of thy seed, to love the Lord thy God with all thine heart, and with all thy soul, that thou mayest live.

As we mature in Christ, we need to ask God Holy Spirit to give us a heart check-up.

A couple of years ago, I found out my father had blockage in the arteries near his heart. Before they could unblock the arteries, a procedure was done called a Cardiac catheterization to examine how well his heart was working. True enough that was in his physical body, but we as Believers need this procedure in our spirit man.

1 Samuel 2:1
And Hannah prayed, and said, My heart rejoiceth in the Lord, mine horn is exalted in the Lord: my mouth is enlarged over mine enemies; because I rejoice in thy salvation.

The Word of God is our cardiac catheter.

Hebrews 4:12 NLT
For the word of God is alive and powerful. It is sharper than the sharpest two-edged sword, cutting between soul and spirit, between joint and marrow. It exposes our innermost thoughts and desires.

Our hearts should be in tune with God's heart.

John 14:1
Let not your heart be troubled: ye believe in God, believe also in me.

When our heart is troubled it sends signals. We begin to doubt God's Word. We become surly, sarcastic, and pessimistic.

Luke 6:45
A good man out of the good treasure of his heart bringeth forth that which is good; and an evil man out of the evil treasure of his heart bringeth forth that which is evil: for of the abundance of the heart his mouth speaketh.

Be encouraged. There is Hope!! Allow God's Word to transform your heart.

Ezekiel 11:19-20
And I will give them one heart, and I will put a new spirit within you; and I will take the stony heart out of their flesh, and will give them an heart of flesh: That they may walk in my statutes, and keep mine ordinances, and do them: and they shall be my people, and I will be their God.

Ephesians 3:17 NLT
Then Christ will make his home in your hearts as you trust in him. Your roots will grow down into God's love and keep you strong.

Ezekiel 36:26-27
A new heart also will I give you, and a new spirit will I put within you: and I will take away the stony heart out of your flesh, and I will give you an heart of flesh. And I will put my spirit within you, and cause you to walk in my statutes, and ye shall keep my judgments, and do them.

2 Thessalonians 3:5
And the Lord direct your hearts into the love of God, and into the patient waiting for Christ.

The heart matters. Let God Holy Spirit perform your procedure, today.

PRISONER OF HOPE

"I have delivered you from death in a waterless pit because of the covenant I made with you, sealed with blood. Come to the place of safety, all you prisoners, for there is yet hope! I promise right now, I will repay you two mercies for each of your woes!" (Zechariah 9:11-12 TLB).

Have you ever set out to accomplish a task, spend time with family, take a vacation, put some money aside or tried to pay a loan off? Then everything went wrong.

The task was draining your time, energy and finances; the time you planned to spend with family, someone had a nasty attitude and soured the occasion; you've packed for the vacation but one of your family members became sick; or you decided to pay your tithe and put some money aside, then a debt collection notice arrived and all your accounts are frozen until the debt is paid in full.

If this is you, hear ye the Word of the Lord God.

But in that coming day, no weapon turned against you shall succeed, and you will have justice against every courtroom lie. This is the heritage of the servants of the Lord. This is the blessing I have given you, says the Lord. Isaiah 54:17 (TLB)

They are like trees planted along the riverbank, bearing fruit each season. Their leaves never wither, and they prosper in all they do. Psalm 1:3 (NLT)

Don't give up. Don't give in. STAND!!!!!!!!!!

You shall not need to fight in this battle; take your positions, stand still, and see the deliverance of the Lord [Who is] with you, ... 2 Chronicles 20:17 (AMPC)

Stand your ground, putting on the belt of truth and the body armor of God's righteousness. Ephesians 6:14 (NLT)

Pray to me, and I will answer you. I will tell you important secrets you have never heard before. Jeremiah 33:3 (NCV)

And I will restore to you the years that the locust hath eaten, the cankerworm, and the caterpiller, and the palmerworm, ... And ye shall eat in plenty, and be satisfied, and praise the name of the Lord your God, that hath dealt wondrously with you: and my people shall never be ashamed. Joel 2:25-26

Why art thou cast down, O my soul? and why art thou disquieted within me? hope thou in God: for I shall yet praise him, who is the health of my countenance, and my God. Psalm 42:11

Keep Hoping in the Lord. He won't fail.

 For as the rain cometh down, and the snow from heaven, and returneth not thither, but watereth the earth, and maketh it bring forth and bud, that it may give seed to the sower, and bread to the eater: So shall my word be that goeth forth out of my mouth: it shall not return unto me void, but it shall accomplish that which I please, and it shall prosper in the thing whereto I sent it. Isaiah 55:10-11

Keep HOPE alive, the Lord God Almighty is on your side.

Do not be afraid! Be strong, and see how the Lord will save you today. For the enemies (Egyptians) you have seen today, you will never see again. Exodus 14:13 (NLV)

Decide today, to be a Prisoner of HOPE

IS YOUR LIGHT ON?

What is light?
An agent that brightens what was dark or dim.

Light can only be seen in darkness.

And God said, Let there be light: and there was light. And God saw the light, that it was good: and God divided the light from the darkness. Genesis 1:3-4

For God, who said, "Let there be light in the darkness," has made this light shine in our hearts so we could know the glory of God that is seen in the face of Jesus Christ.
2 Corinthians 4:6 NLT

Have you ever entered a room that was totally dark? Nothing can be seen but darkness. Then you flip the light switch on, and darkness is no more.

That's how it is spiritually when a believer walks into a room filled with unbelievers.

For once you were full of darkness, but now you have light from the Lord. So live as people of light! For this light within you produces only what is good and right and true. Ephesians 5:8-9 NLT

It's vitally important for you to stay connected to the power source, Christ Jesus. We are all lights but some of us may shine brighter than others.

You are the light of the world—like a city on a hilltop that cannot be hidden. No one lights a lamp and then puts it under a basket. Instead, a lamp is placed on a stand, where it gives light to everyone in the house. In the same way, let your good deeds shine out for all to see, so that everyone will praise your heavenly Father. Matthew 5:14-16 NLT

While ye have light, believe in the light, that ye may be the children of light. John 12:36

If we mimic Christ Jesus everywhere we go, our Father will be glorified. The world would see love, peace, kindness, joy, patience, and faith in action that they may become persuaded to accept Jesus Christ as their Lord and Savior.

All of you are people who belong to the light, who belong to the day. We do not belong to the night or to the darkness.
1 Thessalonians 5:5 GNT

Is your light on?

THIS IS YOUR SEASON

Ecclesiastes 3:1
To every thing there is a season, and a time to every purpose under the heaven:

In 1 Samuel 18-20, No matter how bad King Saul wanted to kill David, he couldn't. God Almighty had already set a time and a season for David to reign as King.

As it was with David, so it is with you. No matter how bad the enemy want to kill you, destroy you, hinder you, or make you miss the blessing, he can't.

God Almighty says, "My word that goes forth out of My mouth: it shall not return to Me void without producing any effect, useless, but it shall accomplish that which I please and purpose, and it shall prosper in the thing for which I sent it" (Isaiah 55:11 AMPC).

Psalm 27:2-3
When the wicked, even mine enemies and my foes, came upon me to eat up my flesh, they stumbled and fell. Though an host should encamp against me, my heart shall not fear: though war should rise against me, in this will I be confident

Do not give up!!! This is your season. GET READY.

Galatians 6:9 NLT
So let's not get tired of doing what is good. At just the right time we will reap a harvest of blessing if we don't give up.

This is your season to receive ALL the promises of God.
This is your season to reap everything you've sown.

Psalm 126:5 AMPC
They who sow in tears shall reap in joy and singing.

Nothing can stop your season of prosperity, great health, wealth, wholeness, favor, increase, blessings, and miracles.

Christ Jesus says, "According to your faith be it unto you" (Matthew 9:29).

Hebrews 6:13-14
For when God made promise to Abraham, because he could swear by no greater, he sware by himself, Saying, Surely blessing I will bless thee, and multiplying I will multiply thee.

If the enemy is fighting you, hindering you, trying to block you, just know this......YOU ARE ENTERING INTO YOUR SEASON. A season filled with POWER. Do Not Give Up.

You are a threat to the kingdom of darkness. So repeat what our Lord God said, "The Lord rebuke thee, O Satan". Zechariah 3:2

Isaiah 54:17 NASB
"No weapon that is formed against you will prosper;
And every tongue that accuses you in judgment you will condemn. This is the heritage of the servants of the LORD, And their vindication is from Me," declares the LORD.

THIS IS YOUR SEASON

HE HEARS YOU

Psalm 17:6
I have called upon thee, for thou wilt hear me, O God: incline thine ear unto me, and hear my speech.

Have you ever called someone and they didn't answer? I remember when I was a child and my mother would call my brother to come inside. My brother never answered her until her voice changed and she called him by his whole name. My brother would rush through the door in a matter of seconds.

I thank God Almighty, I don't have to call him continuously while getting agitated, for Him to answer me.

Then shall ye call upon me, and ye shall go and pray unto me, and I will hearken unto you. Jeremiah 29:12

Let my prayer come before thee: incline thine ear unto my cry; Psalm 88:2

It's a delight in knowing we can talk to our Father and He hear (listens) to every word. Even the words the mouth don't speak.

Hear my prayer, O Lord, give ear to my supplications: in thy faithfulness answer me, and in thy righteousness. Psalm 143:1

In my distress I cried unto the Lord, and he heard me. Psalm 120:1

Psalm 116:2
Because he hath inclined his ear unto me, therefore will I call upon him as long as I live.

Your praying, seeking, praising, or worshipping is not in vain. I hear God saying, "I hear you".

Call unto me, and I will answer thee, and shew thee great and mighty things, which thou knowest not. Jeremiah 33:3

I sought the LORD, and He answered me, And delivered me from all my fears. Psalm 34:4 NASB

HE HEARS YOU

MY GRACE IS SUFFICIENT

And He said unto me, "My grace is sufficient for thee, for My strength is made perfect in weakness." .... 2 Corinthians 12:9

Then Moses said to the Lord, "Please, Lord, I am not a man of words (eloquent, fluent), neither before nor since You have spoken to Your servant; for I am slow of speech and tongue." Exodus 4:10 (AMP)

As humans, why do we give God excuses? Like God didn't know we stuttered when we talk, we get nervous speaking before people, or we've been hurt by church folks. Hello.... GOD knows.

Have you been slothful in giving, forgiving, encouraging, ministering, meditating on the Life Giving Word, or operating in your spiritual gifts?
Why?
Because like the world, you are focusing on your weakness.

Therefore, come out from among unbelievers, and separate yourselves from them, says the Lord. 2 Corinthians 6:17 (NLT)

Moses gave God an excuse, and God still showed off in his life.

My Grace is Sufficient

Apostle Paul asked God to remove the thorn in his flesh, three times (2 Corinthians 12:7-8), but God responded, "My Grace is sufficient for you (My lovingkindness and My mercy are more than enough - always available - regardless of the situation); for My power is being perfected (and is completed and shows itself most effectively) in your weakness" 2 Corinthians 12:9 (AMP).

What task have God Yeshua given you? Are you making excuses?

With the thorn in his flesh, Apostle Paul wrote majority of the New Testament, he planted churches, ran revivals, and served time in prison. And we have the audacity to inform God of our weakness while forgetting that He's ALL KNOWING.

Not having enough money or food to bless someone is no excuse.

In 1 Kings 17:8 (NLT), God told Prophet Elijah to go to Zarephath, and in that city there will be a widow to provide for him.
She told the Prophet, "I swear by the Lord your God that I don't have a single piece of bread in the house. And I have only a handful of flour left in the jar and a little cooking oil in the bottom of the jug. I was just gathering a few sticks to cook this last meal, and then my son and I will die."
She had an excuse why she couldn't give.
But then, God spoke through the Prophet, "Don't be afraid! Do just what you've said but make a little bread for me first. Then use what's left to prepare a meal for yourself and your son. For the Lord God of Israel says, "There will always be flour and olive oil left in your containers...." (1 Kings 17: 12-14).

Maybe this is you. God Holy Spirit telling you to trust Him, to step out by faith but you're looking at your weakness, insufficiency, or pain.

But I hear our Great Jehovah saying, "My Grace is Sufficient for you. Don't worry about the stutter. Don't worry about the past hurts. Don't worry about the lack of financial support. Don't worry about what you can't do. Don't worry about your past. Just step out in ME. I am more than enough. Give Me your weakness and you take My strength. I've come to give you a rich and satisfying life. Now receive My Grace. Receive My Favor. Receive My Strength."

My Grace is Sufficient

HE LOVES YOU

But God is so rich in mercy, and he loved us so much, that even though we were dead because of our sins, he gave us life when he raised Christ from the dead. (It is only by God's grace that you have been saved!) Ephesians 2:4-5 NLT

Have you ever thought about God's love for you? There's nothing you can do to add to or take away from God's love. God's love is everlasting and it never changes.

"For God so loved the world, that He gave His only begotten Son, that whoever believes in Him shall not perish, but have eternal life. John 3:16 NASB

I thank God Almighty for not giving up on mankind in the garden of Eden. But His compassion for us is so great that He gave His only begotten Son to become sin for us.

But God shows and clearly proves His own love for us by the fact that while we were still sinners, Christ (the Messiah, the Anointed One) died for us.
Romans 5:8 AMPC

It is because of the Lord's mercy and loving-kindness that we are not consumed, because His tender compassions fail not.
Lamentations 3:22 AMPC

God's Love validates us as children of the Most High King. We must learn to rest in His Love for us.

Know this, God loves you.

LET HIS POWER WORK IN YOU

Ephesians 3:20 AMPC
Now to Him Who, by (in consequence of) the action of His power that is at work within us, is able to carry out His purpose and do superabundantly, far over and above all that we dare ask or think infinitely beyond our highest prayers, desires, thoughts, hopes, or dreams--

In every super hero movie, each hero has power but also have a weakness. But in us (The Believers), we have the All Power-FULL One (God Holy Spirit) working in us and in Him we have no weakness.

We have the Power to dream beyond our means. Have you dreamt, anything lately?

Acts 1:8 AMPC
But you shall receive power (ability, efficiency, and might) when the Holy Spirit has come upon you, and you shall be My witnesses in Jerusalem and all Judea and Samaria and to the ends (the very bounds) of the earth.

Growing up we use to sing, "Stand up and be a witness". Have you received the Power since you believed? If the answer is yes, it's time to put on your armour and be a witness of who Jesus Christ the Holy One is.

Deuteronomy 8:18 AMPC
But you shall earnestly remember the Lord your God, for it is He Who gives you power to get wealth, that He may establish His covenant which He swore to your fathers, as it is this day.

There is a standard, God Holy Spirit is trying to get us to come up to. This standard goes beyond the status quo. It goes beyond just being saved on your way to heaven. This standard is to have our heart beat in sync with the cadence of God's heart beat. When we come up to this standard, we don't have to work to try to make ends meet. We don't have to toil. We don't have to live a mediocre life. But we know who we are in Christ and we can live that life Jesus spoke of in John 10:10 (MSG), "I came so they can have real and eternal life, more and better life than they ever dreamed of."

Psalm 62:11
God hath spoken once; twice have I heard this; that power belongeth unto God.

God's desire for us is so far and beyond our greatest imagination. And you know what? God want to activate His power in us by faith and we walk there-in.

It's a matter of relationship, not religion. When we pray, we get power. When we fast, we get power. When we commune, share, talk, and listen with Him, we get power.

We must Relinquish control and let God Holy Spirit lead us.

Don't live in your power but live in His Power.

For as many as are led by the Spirit of God, they are the sons of God. Romans 8:14

Galatians 2:20 NET
I have been crucified with Christ, and it is no longer I who live, but Christ lives in me. So the life I now live in the body, I live because of the faithfulness of the Son of God, who loved me and gave himself for me.

Romans 15:13 NET
Now may the God of hope fill you with all joy and peace as you believe in him, so that you may abound in hope by the power of the Holy Spirit.

Let His power work in you

You've Been Set Up

Jeremiah 1:5
Before I formed thee in the belly I knew thee; and before thou camest forth out of the womb I sanctified thee, and I ordained thee a prophet unto the nations.

In 1 Samuel 16 the Prophet Samuel was told by God to anoint the next King. While some was looking at the physique of the man, God was looking at the heart. David, a young boy watching over sheep was setup by a God Almighty.

The same is true with you. Everyone counted you out. You weren't invited to the celebration but that's okay. God has set you up for a blessing that will bless your seed's seed.

Ephesians 1:3 TLB
How we praise God, the Father of our Lord Jesus Christ, who has blessed us with every blessing in heaven because we belong to Christ.

Psalm 84:11
......no good thing will he withhold from them that walk uprightly.

Proverbs 10:6-7
Blessings are upon the head of the just.... The memory of the just is blessed: ....

Saul was set up in Acts chapter 9, when he thought he was going to continue to persecute the saints, But the King of kings showed up and blew Saul's mind. Saul was set up and now we call him Apostle Paul.

Get ready... God Almighty has set you up.

Psalm 23:5-6 NLT
You prepare a feast for me in the presence of my enemies. You honor me by anointing my head with oil. My cup overflows with blessings. Surely your goodness and unfailing love will pursue me all the days of my life, and I will live in the house of the LORD forever.

Psalm 86:17 NET
Show me evidence of your favor! Then those who hate me will see it and be ashamed, for you, O LORD, will help me and comfort me.

You've been set up

TAKE THE WATER OF LIFE FREELY

Water - A chemical compound that every living system need to survive.

Up to 60% of the adult human body is made of water.

In the natural, Water is a vital necessity in our life.

Jesus answered and said unto her, Whosoever drinketh of this water shall thirst again: But whosoever drinketh of the water that I shall give him shall never thirst; but the water that I shall give him shall be in him a well of water springing up into everlasting life. John 4:13-14

Have you ever been thirsty? You tried everything but nothing could quench your thirst. All You wanted was a glass of ice water. It's cool, refreshing and it hits the spot with zero calories.

Christ Jesus offers you His water and it quenches your thirst, heals your body, revives your soul, sends refreshment to your spirit, it gives insight and outlook, it gives you purpose, and it springs up with everlasting life.

Revelation 22:17 MSG
"Come!" say the Spirit and the Bride. Whoever hears, echo, "Come!" Is anyone thirsty? Come! All who will, come and drink, Drink freely of the Water of Life!

Come, drink from the well of Christ Jesus. It's filling and nourishment to the body.

Psalm 1:3
And he shall be like a tree planted by the rivers of water, that bringeth forth his fruit in his season; his leaf also shall not wither; and whatsoever he doeth shall prosper.

When we drink of Jesus' water, nothing can stop us from fulfilling our divine destiny.

Psalm 42:1-2
As the hart panteth after the water brooks, so panteth my soul after thee, O God. My soul thirsteth for God, for the living God: ....

Are you thirsty? Are you thirsting for the Living God?

Come, drink.
Take the water of life freely.

HE'S TALKING TO YOU

John 14:27
Peace I leave with you, my peace I give unto you: not as the world giveth, give I unto you. Let not your heart be troubled, neither let it be afraid.

I thank Jesus, for making this statement because it carries a lot of weight.

No matter what's going on around me, I have His peace. The medical report may be unfavorable but I Have His peace. Finances may be low and employment downsizing but I have His peace.

John 20:21
Then said Jesus to them again, Peace be unto you: as my Father hath sent me, even so send I you.

Peace is only affective during confusion, turbulence, problems, calamity, disturbance, war, or violence. Jesus gives us His peace because He know what we have to face. His peace gives us HOPE.

Mark 4:37-39
And there arose a great storm of wind, and the waves beat into the ship, so that it was now full. And he was in the hinder part of the ship, asleep on a pillow: and they awake him, and say unto him, Master, carest thou not that we perish? And he arose, and rebuked the wind, and said unto the sea, Peace, be still. And the wind ceased, and there was a great calm.

Are you going through a storm in your life? The winds and seas are tossing you. Stand in Jesus' Words... Peace, be still.

Speak to that storm. Speak to that wind. Speak to those waves. PEACE, BE STILL!!!

Jesus Christ is talking to you, receive my PEACE. I give you My Peace.

LORD JESUS BREATHE ON ME
AND SET ME ON FIRE

Luke 3:15-16
And as the people were in expectation, and all men mused in their hearts of John, whether he were the Christ, or not; John answered, saying unto them all, I indeed baptize you with water; but one mightier than I cometh, the latchet of whose shoes I am not worthy to unloose: he shall baptize you with the Holy Ghost and with fire:

In the fairytale world, there are fire breathing dragons. They burn up everything that's a threat to their existence. When they open their mouth, hot scorching fire comes out and destroys everything around them.

Just Imagine, Being baptized (Submerged) in God Holy Spirit and with fire. When the enemy try to hinder you, you open your mouth and the fire of God Holy Spirit destroy all his plots, plans, tactics and vices.

Just imagine, all your friendly enemies that smile in your face but despise your very existence. But you being FULL of God Holy Spirit, have the power to love them unconditionally.

God Holy Spirit is POWER and FIRE.

Yes, He's more than that but for this devotion we are meditating on these attributes.

John 20:21-22
Then said Jesus to them again, Peace be unto you: as my Father hath sent me, even so send I you. And when he had said this, he breathed on them, and saith unto them, Receive ye the Holy Ghost:

Imagine, You going through hard times, and you feel like giving up. Christ Jesus says, "Peace be unto you (say your name)". Then He breathe on you and say, "Receive ye God Holy Spirit (The Comforter, Dunamas, Miraculous Power).

Have ye received the Holy Ghost since ye believed?
Acts 19:2

Avail yourself for another in-filling. Avail yourself to be baptized again.

I hear God Holy Spirit saying, "open thy mouth wide, and I will fill it" (Psalm 81:10).

Christ Jesus is ready to breathe on you. Get in position. Get ready for the out pour. Receive God Holy Spirit, now.

COME EAT

Isaiah 1:19
If ye be willing and obedient, ye shall eat the good of the land:

After hours of prepping and cooking, my mother would make a loud call to the family, "Dinner is ready. Come eat".
My siblings and I would rush to the restroom to wash up for dinner. Excited and hungry some would rush down the stairs but my younger brother and I would jump down seven steps with hopes to land on our feet. I have a large family, so my parents and my older siblings sat at the main dinner table, while my younger brother and I sat at our table (The children's table).
When I got to my seat, all I had to do was sit down. My mother had the table prepared.... the plate, the fork, knife, and spoon, the napkin, and the glass. She also put a plate of bread on each table.

True enough this dinner was to refresh our flesh (The natural man) but God our Father has prepared a table and ready to serve His food, to refresh our spirit man.

Psalm 23:5 MSG
You serve me a six-course dinner right in front of my enemies.
....

Just as we hunger in the natural we also hunger in the spirit. With the natural man we feed it 2, 3, 4, and maybe 5 times a day. But how often do we feed our spirit man?

Psalm 22:26
The meek shall eat and be satisfied: they shall praise the Lord that seek him: your heart shall live for ever.

Luke 4:4
And Jesus answered him, saying, It is written, That man shall not live by bread alone, but by every word of God.

Your natural man may be fat and well fed but your spirit man may be deprived and malnourished.

God Yeshua has prepared everything (The living Word, the sacrifice, the Living Water, healing, peace, The Comforter) for our spirit man. All we have to do is go to the table.

The Saints of old use to sing, "Come over here, where the table is spread and the feast of the Lord is going on. There's joy over here. There's peace over here".

We need to accept their invitation and run to the table.

Jesus is saying, "Come unto me, all ye that labour and are heavy laden, and I will give you rest. Take my yoke upon you, and learn of me; for I am meek and lowly in heart: and ye shall find rest unto your souls. For my yoke is easy, and my burden is light" (Matthew 11:28-30).

Jesus is calling, "Dinner is ready. Come eat."

Come to be refreshed. Come to be revived and renewed.
Come to fellowship with God.
Just Come.

Everything God Almighty has prepared I guarantee, you will enjoy.

Psalm 34:8
O taste and see that the Lord is good: blessed is the man that trusteth in him.

Come eat!!! You don't have to RSVP. Just come.

YOU ARE VICTORIOUS

2 Corinthians 2:14
Now thanks be unto God, which always causeth us to triumph in Christ, and maketh manifest the savour of his knowledge by us in every place.

Psalm 41:11
By this I know that thou favourest me, because mine enemy doth not triumph over me.

Because of God's Love for us, we live in VICTORY. It doesn't matter what it looks like. It doesn't matter what they say. Just know, God Almighty ALWAYS causes us to triumph and He calls us victorious, winners, over-comers, more than conquerors, in Christ Jesus.

2 Samuel 22:36 NLT
You have given me your shield of victory; your help has made me great.

Psalm 3:8 NLT
Victory comes from you, O LORD. May you bless your people.

Psalm 18:35 NLT
You have given me your shield of victory. Your right hand supports me; your help has made me great.

God has already given you the victory!! Heaven backs you up. Now tell yourself, "I HAVE THE VICTORY".

No matter the circumstance, problem, report, or what others may say......YOU HAVE THE VICTORY.

Psalm 62:1 NLT
I wait quietly before God, for my victory comes from him.

Psalm 118:21 NLT
I thank you for answering my prayer and giving me victory!

Psalm 149:4 NLT
For the LORD delights in his people; he crowns the humble with victory.

Rise up and know

You are VICTORIOUS!!!!

IN THE ABSENCE OF........
I STILL BELIEVE!!!!!!!!

Hebrews 11:1
Now faith is the substance of things hoped for, the evidence of things not seen.

Hebrews 11:6
But without faith it is impossible to please him: for he that cometh to God must believe that he is, and that he is a rewarder of them that diligently seek him.

Have you been waiting on a promise to be manifested in your life?

Do Not Give Up!!

Isaiah 55:11 NASB
So will My word be which goes forth from My mouth; It will not return to Me empty, Without accomplishing what I desire, And without succeeding in the matter for which I sent it.

I hear God Holy Spirit saying, "I DO NOT LIE. IF I SAID IT. IF I SHOWED YOU. BELIEVE ME. IT SHALL COME TO MANIFESTATION ".

In the absence of a son, Sara still believed God. Hebrews 11:11

In the absence of a sacrifice, Abraham still believed God. Hebrews 11:17-19

James 2:23
And the scripture was fulfilled which saith, Abraham believed God, and it was imputed unto him for righteousness: and he was called the Friend of God.

In the absence of wholeness, the woman with the issue of blood, believed if she touch the hem of Jesus' garment, she would be made whole. (Matt 9:20, Mark 5:25, Luke 8:43-44)

In the absence of food, 5,000 men plus women and children were fed with 2 fish and 5 loaves. Mark 6:41

Jeremiah 32:27
Behold, I am the Lord, the God of all flesh: is there any thing too hard for me?

Hebrews 6:13-15
For when God made promise to Abraham, because he could swear by no greater, he sware by himself, Saying, Surely blessing I will bless thee, and multiplying I will multiply thee. And so, after he had patiently endured, he obtained the promise.

1 John 5:14-15
And this is the confidence that we have in him, that, if we ask any thing according to his will, he heareth us: And if we know that he hear us, whatsoever we ask, we know that we have the petitions that we desired of him.

Keep your faith alive.

BELIEVE GOD

SAY TO THIS MOUNTAIN

Years ago, many people use to sing these songs, "I'm coming up on the rough side of the mountain" and "Lord, don't move the mountain give me the strength to climb". But Jesus said, "ye shall say unto this mountain, Be thou removed, and be thou cast into the sea; it shall be done" (Matthew 21:21).

Jesus had already given us authority and He want us to stand in faith, knowing if we didn't waver it will happen.

Religion would have you to tolerate sickness, disease, trials, storms, and foolishness but relationship with Jesus Christ says to you, "I am come that you might have life, and that you might have it more abundantly" (John 10:10).

Say to this mountain.

When the disciples were on the boat and the seas were raging, and after they had tolerated it long enough then they cried out to Jesus. "And he arose, and rebuked the wind, and said unto the sea, Peace, be still. And the wind ceased, and there was a great calm. And he said unto them, Why are ye so fearful? how is it that ye have no faith?" (Mark 4:39-40)

Use God's Word as an act of Faith.

After Mary and Martha cried over the death of Lazarus, even after Jesus told them, "he sleepeth", they still didn't believe.

John 11:40
Jesus saith unto her (Martha), Said I not unto thee, that, if thou wouldest believe, thou shouldest see the glory of God?

Then they took away the stone from the place where the dead was laid. And Jesus lifted up his eyes, and said, Father, I thank thee that thou hast heard me. And I knew that thou hearest me always: but because of the people which stand by I said it, that they may believe that thou hast sent me. John 11:41-42

Jesus used His Words.
"Father, I thank thee that thou hast heard me. And I knew that thou hearest me always".

Use God's Word and you will see miracles performed.

And this is the confidence that we have in him, that, if we ask any thing according to his will, he heareth us: And if we know that he hear us, whatsoever we ask, we know that we have the petitions that we desired of him. 1 John 5:14-15

Say to the mountain in your life, "Be thou removed, and be thou cast into the sea".

Say to the raging seas and the mighty storm in your life, "Peace be still".

For verily I say unto you, That whosoever shall say unto this mountain, Be thou removed, and be thou cast into the sea; and shall not doubt in his heart, but shall believe that those things which he saith shall come to pass; he shall have whatsoever he saith. Mark 11:23

In other words, Jesus is saying, "Stop doubting and just believe. Whatever you say will happen".

You're not living this life to tolerate stuff but to speak in faith to change the world for the better.

Remember you are a Kingdom builder.

Say to this mountain

YOUR DAY IS COMING

Luke 18:1-8
And he spake a parable unto them to this end, that men ought always to pray, and not to faint; Saying, There was in a city a judge, which feared not God, neither regarded man: And there was a widow in that city; and she came unto him, saying, Avenge me of mine adversary. And he would not for a while: but afterward he said within himself, Though I fear not God, nor regard man; Yet because this widow troubleth me, I will avenge her, lest by her continual coming she weary me. And the Lord said, Hear what the unjust judge saith. And shall not God avenge his own elect, which cry day and night unto him, though he bear long with them? I tell you that he will avenge them speedily. Nevertheless when the Son of man cometh, shall he find faith on the earth?

Some of you been praying and believing for a situation to change, but I have a Word from God just for you.

Your Day is Coming sooner than you think.

For God is not unrighteous to forget your work and labour of love, which ye have shewed toward his name, in that ye have ministered to the saints, and do minister. Hebrews 6:10

1 Peter 3:12
For the eyes of the Lord are over the righteous, and his ears are open unto their prayers: ......

If the unjust judge knew that God listens to his saints and avenges them quickly, we should be filled with confidence that God will answer.

Revelation 5:8 AMPC
And when He had taken the scroll, the four living creatures
and the twenty-four elders of the heavenly Sanhedrin
prostrated themselves before the Lamb. Each was holding a
harp (lute or guitar), and they had golden bowls full of incense
(fragrant spices and gums for burning), which are the prayers
of God's people (the saints).

.

Revelation 8:3-4
And another angel came and stood at the altar, having a
golden censer; and there was given unto him much incense,
that he should offer it with the prayers of all saints upon the
golden altar which was before the throne. And the smoke of
the incense, which came with the prayers of the saints,
ascended up before God out of the angel's hand.

Your Day is Coming, sooner than you think.

HE HATH ANOINTED ME

The Spirit of the Lord is upon me, because he hath anointed me to preach the gospel to the poor; he hath sent me to heal the brokenhearted, to preach deliverance to the captives, and recovering of sight to the blind, to set at liberty them that are bruised, To preach the acceptable year of the Lord. (Luke 4:18-19)

Christ Jesus was in Nazareth in the Synagogue on the Sabbath, when He opened the book of the Prophet Esaias, and read the above scripture.

Jesus Christ our Savior knew His calling and walked powerfully in His gifts. He said,
"The Spirit of the Lord is upon me, because he hath anointed me to.....".

My question is......
What have God Holy Spirit anointed you to do?

Are you walking, working, operating in that anointing?

Jesus Christ is our great example. He didn't try to mimic any one, He knew Who He was. He wasn't trying to operate in someone else's gift but He worked His gift.

Reading the above scripture let me know, that when we work, operate and walk in the anointing God Holy Spirit has saturated us in, we don't have to make anything happen. People will be blessed, delivered, and set free because we are led by God Holy Spirit and we are operating through Him.

Jesus said, "I am anointed to Preach, Heal, Deliver, Recover sight, set at Liberty, and Preach the favorable year of the Lord".

Ask yourself, "What am I anointed to do?"

You are not anointed to be a slave.
You are not anointed to be someone else.
You are not anointed to operate in someone else's gift.

In 1 Samuel 17, Goliath defied The Lord God of Israel. While the army of Israel was frightened by Goliath's size and his threatening remarks, there arose a lad that knew who he was and who God Almighty is. David, was on a mission to deliver food to his brothers. He heard the disrespectful remarks of the uncircumcised Philistine. In Verses 38 and 39, King Saul armed David with his armor. But David, a small lad couldn't fit this bulky armor that's fit for a grown man. So David went in God's Anointing.

David knew his gifts and what he was anointed for.

Because he didn't try to be like his brothers, King Saul, or the other soldiers, he fought in the anointing of God Almighty and defeated Goliath and the Philistines.

You are anointed to be you!!!

This is why I remind you to fan into flames the spiritual gift God gave you .... 2 Timothy 1:6 NLT

If you are a preacher, preach under the anointing with passion and love.

If you are a teacher, study and then teach under the anointing with enthusiasm and clarity.

If you are a psalmist, sing under the anointing that the Angels want to sing with you.

It's the anointing that destroys the yoke but we must know what we are anointed for.

Father God in Jesus Christ, forgive me for not operating, working, and walking in the anointing you have for me. Give me the confidence in You to know who I am in You so that I can touch the world. I give You, O Lord, all glory and honor. And it is so In Jesus Christ. Amen.

He Hath Anointed me

I SHALL NOT BE MOVED

Psalm 16:8 AMPC
I have set the Lord continually before me; because He is at my right hand, I shall not be moved.

Sometimes in life, our faith is challenged but we must STAND in God's Word and say, "I shall not be moved".

Psalm 1:3
And he shall be like a tree planted by the rivers of water...

Sickness, disease, heartbreak, death of a loved one, financial issues, problem children, and marriage issues, may try to invade the boundaries of your faith but you must encourage yourself with God's Word.

1 Peter 1:6-7 NLT
So be truly glad. There is wonderful joy ahead, even though you must endure many trials for a little while. These trials will show that your faith is genuine. It is being tested as fire tests and purifies gold-though your faith is far more precious than mere gold. So when your faith remains strong through many trials, it will bring you much praise and glory and honor on the day when Jesus Christ is revealed to the whole world.

In 1 Samuel, David was on the run from Saul. David had an opportunity to kill Saul and his men but David was secure in God's promise. His faith seen him through.

Psalm 62:2
He only is my rock and my salvation; he is my defence; I shall not be greatly moved.

I hear God Holy Spirit saying, "Fear ye not, stand still, and see the salvation of the Lord, which he will shew to you to day: for the Egyptians (the enemy) whom ye have seen to day, ye shall see them again no more for ever" (Exodus 14:13).

As you go about your day, remind yourself, "I shall not be moved". God rescued you when He sent His only begotten Son, and He will do it again. Hold on and keep the faith.

Psalm 16:8
I have set the Lord always before me: because he is at my right hand, I shall not be moved.

CAN JESUS SEE YOUR FAITH?

Matthew 9:2,6-7
And, behold, they brought to him a man sick of the palsy, lying on a bed: and Jesus seeing their faith said unto the sick of the palsy; Son, be of good cheer; thy sins be forgiven thee. Arise, take up thy bed, and go unto thine house. And he arose, and departed to his house.

We know what the scriptures say about faith, but what does our actions say.

James 1:22
But be ye doers of the word, and not hearers only, deceiving your own selves.

In Mark 2:2-4 The friends of this man saw that there was no room to bring their friend, which was on a bed, in.
One of them had a brilliant idea to go through the roof.
The scripture never tells the size of the man on the bed but it tells us his friends carried him.

Just imagine, Jesus preaching about God's redeeming love, and the ceiling starts to cave in. Clay falling upon the heads of those sitting and listening. And all of a sudden, when the people looked up they saw the sun shining in. The four friends removed the roof to lower their friend down to where Jesus was.

What are you doing, for Jesus to see your faith?

James 2:17
Even so faith, if it hath not works, is dead, being alone.

In 1 Samuel 1:5-27 It tells of Hannah being barren. Yes, she cried, but she put action with her tears that showed God her faith and that faith produced a Mighty Man of Valor; Prophet Samuel.

Can your faith be seen?

It's great to believe God for a job but you must do your part. Prepare your resume, download it to various employment engines, fine tune your skills, and do follow-up calls to the companies you applied to.

You believing God for healing is great. But have you started eating healthy? Are you exercising? Are you drinking 64 ounces or more of water. Are you getting enough sleep?

For your faith to be seen you must be in motion also. God has done His part now you must do yours.

The woman with the issue of blood didn't stop with the bad reports. She was determined she was going to be healed. She spoke faith to herself. Then she put actions with her faith and got the results she was believing for; healing.

James 2:14
What doth it profit, my brethren, though a man say he hath faith, and have not works? can faith save him?

Can Jesus see your FAITH?

LORD, HELP THOU MINE UNBELIEF

Matthew 13:58
And he did not many mighty works there because of their unbelief.

Matthew 17:20
And Jesus said unto them, Because of your unbelief: for verily I say unto you, If ye have faith as a grain of mustard seed, ye shall say unto this mountain, Remove hence to yonder place; and it shall remove; and nothing shall be impossible unto you.

Being human is hard. We are taught as children to trust our sensory system (sight, hearing, touch, smell, and taste). As adults we still trust in this system and then we receive Jesus Christ as our Lord and Savior.

I've learned, faith uses one of the senses and is a learned behavior. We must be willing to hear in order for faith to be activated.

Romans 10:17
So then faith cometh by hearing, and hearing by the word of God.

Mark 9:23-24
Jesus said unto him, If thou canst believe, all things are possible to him that believeth. And straightway the father of the child cried out, and said with tears, Lord, I believe; help thou mine unbelief.

I thank Jesus Christ for knowing that faith is activated by hearing. This father wanted his son healed and delivered. The disciples tried but failed.

But Jesus, being gentle in spirit, said to the father, "If thou canst believe, all things are possible to him that believeth" (Mark 9:23).

Like this father, some of us need a miracle. Maybe it's your children, your marriage, your finances, your career, or a physical healing. I encourage you to sincerely cry out, Lord, I believe; help thou mine unbelief.

He's listening. He cares. He wants to help.

Lord, I believe; help thou mine unbelief.

I hear God Holy Spirit saying, "Ask for my help. I want to give you those hidden desires that you haven't shared with anyone. I want to bless you so, that your enemies stand in total awe of My Goodness. Let me help you. Let me show off in you. Let me show off in that situation. Let me be your God of Miracles". And it is so. In Jesus Christ. Amen.

OH NO, I'LL NEVER FORGET

Psalm 3:1-3
LORD, how they have increased who trouble me! Many are they who rise up against me. Many are they who say of me, "There is no help for him in God." Selah   But You, O LORD, are a shield for me, My glory and the One who lifts up my head.

Every believer can use this verse as their testimony, for the Lord rescued each of us from our enemies, sickness, death, and even the harm we could've done to ourselves.

Oh no, I'll never forget

Psalm 18:6
In my distress I called upon the LORD, And cried out to my God; He heard my voice from His temple, And my cry came before Him, even to His ears.

Can you look back over your life and see how far you've come? How your enemy said you wouldn't make it. How the loan officer said, you would never be able to afford that house. How your friendly enemies said, you would never amount to anything. BUT GOD!!!

It was the Lord God that heard your cry. It was the Lord God that snatched you from hell's gates. It was the Lord God, that protected you from the noisome pestilence. It was the Lord God that raised you to show you His favor.

Oh no, I'll never forget.

Psalm 107:19-21

Then they cried out to the LORD in their trouble, And He saved them out of their distresses. He sent His word and healed them, And delivered them from their destructions. Oh, that men would give thanks to the LORD for His goodness, And for His wonderful works to the children of men!

Do you remember when the Lord God healed you? It wasn't the prescription drugs; it was God's healing anointing. When the doctors gave you bad news, God sent His Word and now you're living a healthy life in victory.

Oh no, I'll never forget.

Psalm 119:16
I will delight myself in Your statutes; I will not forget Your word.

Life happens but the word God spoke over you will come to pass. He didn't forget so don't you forget.

Psalm 119:49-50 NET
Remember your word to your servant, for you have given me hope. This is what comforts me in my trouble, for your promise revives me.

Oh no, I'll never forget.

Psalm 40:2
He brought me up also out of an horrible pit, out of the miry clay, and set my feet upon a rock, and established my goings.

Oh no, I'll never forget.

Take time right now to give the Lord God praise. He's worthy of all glory and honor. Let Him know, "Lord God, I'll never forget what You've done for me".

Hallelujah

FILL ME, OH LORD

Isaiah 6:1
In the year that king Uzziah died I saw also the Lord sitting upon a throne, high and lifted up, and his train filled the temple.

As I meditate on this verse, I hear myself whispering, "Fill me, Oh Lord".

I quickly reflect to the following scriptures:

1 Corinthians 3:16
Know ye not that ye are the temple of God, and that the Spirit of God dwelleth in you?

1 Corinthians 6:19
What? know ye not that your body is the temple of the Holy Ghost which is in you, which ye have of God, and ye are not your own?

If our body is the temple of God Holy Spirit, can we ask Him to let His train (The gloriousness of His spirit which is the total embodiment of Himself) fill us (The temple) to the fullness there of?

In the book of Acts which is the acts of God Holy Spirit, 2:4, it says, "And they were all filled with the Holy Ghost, and began to speak with other tongues, as the Spirit gave them utterance".

Have you ever yearned so great (In abundance) for God, that you couldn't eat or sleep? But all you wanted to do was bask in His presence. You didn't want to ask for anything, all you wanted was to be filled to the overflowing with His spirit.

This is what happened to Isaiah. Someone had to die in his life for him to recognize the spiritualness of God.

What is the thing that has to die in your life for you to recognize the power of God? Do you have to experience a bad marriage? Loss of employment? Financial hardship? Sickness? Separation or departing of friendship?

Say with me, "Fill me, Oh Lord".

Acts 4:31
And when they had prayed, the place was shaken where they were assembled together; and they were all filled with the Holy Ghost, and they spake the word of God with boldness.

In the above chapter, the Saints were threatened by the priests, and the captain of the temple, and the Sadducees, for preaching and teaching Jesus and His resurrection. This is what led them to boldly pray.

But when they prayed, not only was the place shaken, but they were filled with God Holy Spirit.

Fill me, Oh Lord.

Ephesians 3:19
And to know the love of Christ, which passeth knowledge, that ye might be filled with all the fulness of God.

Colossians 1:9
For this cause we also, since the day we heard it, do not cease to pray for you, and to desire that ye might be filled with the knowledge of his will in all wisdom and spiritual understanding;

I hunger and yearn for God Almighty to fill me to the overflow. I encourage you to get hungry and thirsty for God. Jesus told us, "All that the Father giveth me shall come to me; and him that cometh to me I will in no wise cast out" (John 6:37). You will not be turned away or denied when you want more of God Holy Spirit.

Jesus said in:

Matthew 5:6, "Blessed are they which do hunger and thirst after righteousness: for they shall be filled."

Luke 6:21, "Blessed are ye that hunger now: for ye shall be filled."

John 6:35, "I am the bread of life: he that cometh to me shall never hunger; and he that believeth on me shall never thirst."

Don't wait for tragedy to happen in your life that will make you see the spiritualness of God, but desire Him above all others and then you can see Him in the splendor of His Power.

Fill me, Oh Lord.

HE IS WORTHY

2 Samuel 22:2-4
.....The Lord is my rock, and my fortress, and my deliverer; The God of my rock; in him will I trust: he is my shield, and the horn of my salvation, my high tower, and my refuge, my saviour; thou savest me from violence. I will call on the Lord, who is worthy to be praised: so shall I be saved from mine enemies.

As I read David's song to the Lord, I join in, saying, "HE is Worthy". King David and I may not have the same testimony but we can sing in unison, "Lord, You are Worthy".

Revelation 4:11
Thou art worthy, O Lord, to receive glory and honour and power: for thou hast created all things, and for thy pleasure they are and were created.

You don't have to wait to join Heaven's choir, you can sing now, "Hallelujah, Lord, You are Worthy".

Revelation 5:13 AMPC
And I heard every created thing in heaven and on earth and under the earth in Hades, the place of departed spirits and on the sea and all that is in it, crying out together, To Him Who is seated on the throne and to the Lamb be ascribed the blessing and the honor and the majesty (glory, splendor) and the power (might and dominion) forever and ever (through the eternities of the eternities)!

Have the Lord God ever brought you out?
Did He open doors for you?
Have He healed your body?
Is He your refuge and strength?

Open your mouth and say with me, "Hallelujah! Lord, You are Worthy".

Jeremiah 10:10,12-13 AMPC
But the Lord is the true God and the God of truth (the God Who is Truth). He is the living God and the everlasting King. At His wrath the earth quakes, and the nations are not able to bear His indignation. God made the earth by His power; He established the world by His wisdom and by His understanding and skill stretched out the heavens. When He utters His voice, there is a tumult of waters in the heavens, and He causes the vapors to ascend from the ends of the earth. He makes lightnings for the rain and brings forth the wind out from His treasuries and from His storehouses.

The Lord God Almighty, gave us everything we need to live in this earth. He deserves ALL Glory, Honor, and Praise.

In 2 Samuel 6:16-21, I understand why King David went crazy in praising God and didn't care who observed him. He was acknowledging the Lord God and letting Him know, "Lord, You are Worthy".

What can you do today to let God know He is Worthy of all praise, worship, glory, honor, and adoration?

Let me make a suggestion. Put praise on your lips and worship in your heart and do like King David, go crazy in the Lord.

Hallelujah

HE IS WORTHY!!!

Psalm 150:6 Let every thing that hath breath praise the Lord. Praise ye the Lord.

JOIN IN

Revelation 4:8-11
And the four beasts had each of them six wings about him; and they were full of eyes within: and they rest not day and night, saying, Holy, holy, holy, Lord God Almighty, which was, and is, and is to come. And when those beasts give glory and honour and thanks to him that sat on the throne, who liveth for ever and ever, The four and twenty elders fall down before him that sat on the throne, and worship him that liveth for ever and ever, and cast their crowns before the throne, saying, Thou art worthy, O Lord, to receive glory and honour and power: for thou hast created all things, and for thy pleasure they are and were created.

Just imagine, worshipping God Almighty 24 hours a day, every day. It would be an honor and pleasure to worship the King of kings.

One of the many things I love about God Almighty, is that I don't have to wait to get to Heaven. I can worship Him now.

Revelation 11:16-17
And the four and twenty elders, which sat before God on their seats, fell upon their faces, and worshipped God, Saying, We give thee thanks, O Lord God Almighty, which art, and wast, and art to come; because thou hast taken to thee thy great power, and hast reigned.

As I read about the worship that's going on in Heaven, I get excited and over joyed but then I join in and get caught up. I get so caught up, all my cares and concerns are driven away and all my burdens are lifted. Why?

Glory and honour are in his presence; strength and gladness are in his place. 1 Chronicles 16:27

Thou wilt shew me the path of life: in thy presence is fulness of joy; at thy right hand there are pleasures for evermore. Psalm 16:11

Now the Lord is that Spirit: and where the Spirit of the Lord is, there is liberty. 2 Corinthians 3:17

Please don't wait until Sunday to Worship our Lord. He is worthy of Worship now. Every day and all day, our lips should be filled with praise and our spirit in worship to the Lord God Almighty which sits on the throne.

Join in, and Worship

"Holy, holy, holy, is the LORD of hosts: the whole earth is full of his glory" (Isaiah 6:3).

BELIEVE

The prayer of the upright is the Lord's delight.   Proverbs 15:8

The Lord heareth the prayer of the righteous. Proverbs 15:29

Praise be to the Lord, for He has heard my cry for mercy. Psalm 28:6

To You, Lord I called; to the Lord I cried for mercy. Psalm 30:8

I told you my plans, and you answered. Now teach me Your decrees. Psalm 119:26 (NLT)

I took my troubles to the Lord; I cried out to Him, and He answered my prayer. Psalm 120:1 (NLT)

Believe in the prayers you pray and you will see the answers from the God that is moved by your FAITH.

The first rule of prayer is the first rule of faith.........BELIEVE

Jesus said unto him, If thou canst believe, all things are possible to him that believeth. Mark 9:23

I tell you the truth, anyone who believes has eternal life. Yes, I am the bread of life! John 6:47-48

Anyone who believes in me may come and drink! For the Scriptures declare, "Rivers of living water will flow from his heart." John 7:38 (NLT)

In that day you will not [need to] ask Me about anything. I assure you and most solemnly say to you, whatever you ask the Father in My name [as My representative], He will give you. Until now you have not asked [the Father] for anything in My name; but now ask and keep on asking and you will receive, so that your joy may be full and complete. John 16:23-24 (AMP)

Are you ready to experience answered prayers? I encourage you to Believe.

This is the confidence we have in approaching God: that if we ask anything according to his will, he hears us. And if we know that he hears us—whatever we ask—we know that we have what we asked of him. 1 John 5:14-15 (NIV)

Maybe you need to ask yourself, "What is stopping me from believing?"

That's why we must be careful of what and who we listen to. If they not talking FAITH don't listen.

Romans 10:17
So then faith cometh by hearing, and hearing by the word of God.

Is what you listening to, challenging you to believe God Almighty?

Believe that God want to bless you.
Believe that God want to bring you out.
Believe that God is listening every time you utter a prayer.
Believe that God that He will supply whatever it is you need.

Just Believe.

And Abram believed the Lord, and the Lord counted him as righteous because of his faith. Genesis 15:6 (NLT)

RAISE YOUR PRAISE

Psalm 122:1
I was glad when they said unto me, Let us go into the house of the Lord.

King David penned the above verse but I hear it ringing in my ears. With me, I become so excited and filled with joy when it's time to prepare for worship. Please understand, my preparation goes beyond deciding what colors I will adorn myself in but it's preparing my spirit. As a child born in a believer's family, I found out where my strength comes from.

Dahlia had to seduce Samson, for him to reveal the source of his strength but like many of you, I realized that my strength comes from God, serving God, and Praising God.

2 Samuel 22:4 AMPC
I call on the Lord, Who is worthy to be praised, and I am saved from my enemies.

Psalm 9:2
I will be glad and rejoice in thee: I will sing praise to thy name, O thou most High.

My excitement is not entertainment but it's pure praise and Worship to my King of Kings, Lord God Yeshua.

Every level in David's life, there were bigger devils but he knew there was strength and divine power in his praise to The Lord God Almighty.

David raised his praise that his household kicked up their feet against him. They didn't understand his praise because they didn't go through the wilderness with him.

2 Samuel 22:50 AMPC
For this I will give thanks and extol You, O Lord, among the nations; I will sing praises to Your name.

People see you blessed and favored now, but where were they when you were in the wilderness fighting your Goliaths?

Matthew 26:36-40 tells that Jesus went to Gethsemane to pray. Jesus invited Peter, and the two sons of Zebedee; James and John. All Jesus asked them to do was, "sit ye here and watch".

No one will ever understand your praise if they are not willing to go through your wilderness with you.

Psalm 28:7 NLT
The LORD is my strength and shield. I trust him with all my heart. He helps me, and my heart is filled with joy. I burst out in songs of thanksgiving.

Be encouraged

Psalm 33:1
Rejoice in the Lord, O ye righteous: for praise is comely for the upright.

Your level of praise this year should be higher than it was last year.

The song writer said, "When I look back over my life". That's what we need to do. Take a look back. That will make you go crazy, praising God Almighty.

That sickness didn't take you out of here.
That job loss didn't make you lose your mind.
But God turned it, in your favor.
You are now healthy and whole.
You started your own business and it's successful.

Joseph said it best in Genesis 50:20 (NIV), "You intended to harm me, but God intended it for good".

Raise your praise.

Let me wake up Paul and Silas. In Acts chapter 16 we know they were thrown in jail but that didn't stop them. They used their weapons; prayer and praise. Verses 25 and 26 (NIV) says they, "were praying and singing hymns to God, and the other prisoners were listening to them. Suddenly there was such a violent earthquake that the foundations of the prison were shaken. At once all the prison doors flew open, and everyone's chains came loose."

What would happen if you prayed and raised your praise?

I believe everything that was holding you back would be destroyed. Everything that held you in bondage would be destroyed. All the shackles and the chains would crumble. Every plot, plan, tactic, mission, and thought that the enemy tried to send against you would be DESTROYED.

No weapon formed against you shall prosper, And every tongue which rises against you in judgment You shall condemn. Isaiah 54:17 NKJV

Psalm 147:1
Praise ye the Lord: for it is good to sing praises unto our God; for it is pleasant; and praise is comely.

Raise your Praise, for He is Worthy.

I dare you to raise your praise. Instead of complaining, raise your praise. Instead of murmuring, raise your praise. Use your weapons which are prayer and praise, and watch God show up and show out in your life.

Raise your praise.

Testifying Tuesday

Revelation 12:11
And they overcame him by the blood of the Lamb, and by the word of their testimony; and they loved not their lives unto the death.

Remember when we use to have testimony service. We use to share with others about the goodness of the Lord and how He brought us out. How he closed the wrong doors and how He clothed us in our right mind.

Oh how we use to testify and encourage others, by letting them know, If the Lord did it for me, He will do it for you.

Testifying was like a release valve for our soul to praise and magnify the Lord Most High.

Romans 10:17
So then faith cometh by hearing, ……..

Every time we testify, those that hear it start growing in their faith.

When we read the testimonies of the Saints in the Bible, we take courage in knowing, if God did it for them, He will do it for us.

Paul testified about what he was enduring but then he said, "But none of these things move me, neither count I my life dear unto myself, so that I might finish my course with joy, and the ministry, which I have received of the Lord Jesus, to testify the gospel of the grace of God" (Acts 20:24).

Through all the ups and downs in life, Apostle Paul encourages us to continue to testify of the Grace of the Lord God Almighty.

Find someone to share your testimony with. Encourage them in the Faith. Tell of the Lord's goodness and His faithfulness to you. They'll be blessed by your testimony.

This is Testifying Tuesday

ARE YOU A BELIEVER?

Believer is someone who is a devotee, follower, adherent, supporter of one who they believe can bring change, deliver, or set them free.

Do you believe Jesus Christ is the Son of the Living God?

Do you believe He died for your sins and for the sins of the world?

Do you believe God Almighty raised Jesus Christ from the dead?

Genesis 15:6
And he believed in the Lord; and he counted it to him for righteousness.

Psalm 27:13
I had fainted, unless I had believed to see the goodness of the Lord in the land of the living.

Do you believe Jesus can bring you out?

Do you believe God is working all things for your good?

Do you believe that when you give, it shall be given back into you?

Matthew 8:13
And Jesus said unto the centurion, Go thy way; and as thou hast believed, so be it done unto thee.

Matthew 9:28
and Jesus saith unto them, Believe ye that I am able to do this?

Do you believe, Jesus is able to do the impossible in your life?

Mark 9:23
Jesus said unto him, If thou canst believe, all things are possible to him that believeth.

Do you believe whatsoever you ask in prayer according to His Will, He will do it?

Mark 11:24
Therefore I say unto you, What things soever ye desire, when ye pray, believe that ye receive them, and ye shall have them.

Do you believe God can deliver?

Do you believe God will supply all your need?

Do you believe, healing is yours?

Luke 1:45
And blessed is she that believed: for there shall be a performance of those things which were told her from the Lord.

Do you believe your sins are forgiven?

Is it easier to forgive sins, than to bless you and supply all your need?

John 3:12,15
If I have told you earthly things, and ye believe not, how shall ye believe, if I tell you of heavenly things? That whosoever believeth in me should not perish, but have eternal life.

John 3:36
He that believeth on the Son hath everlasting life: and he that believeth not the Son shall not see life; but the wrath of God abideth on him.

John 6:47
Verily, verily, I say unto you, He that believeth on me hath everlasting life.

By My stripes you are healed.

Are you a BELIEVER?

What's stopping you from believing God to supply, deliver, heal, provide, favor, increase, strengthen, or make whole?

Maybe it's time for a BELIEVER check-up.

Are you a believer?

TESTIFYING MONDAY

1 Chronicles 29:10-13
Wherefore David blessed the Lord before all the congregation: and David said, "Blessed be thou, Lord God of Israel our father, for ever and ever. Thine, O Lord, is the greatness, and the power, and the glory, and the victory, and the majesty: for all that is in the heaven and in the earth is thine; thine is the kingdom, O Lord, and thou art exalted as head above all. Both riches and honour come of thee, and thou reignest over all; and in thine hand is power and might; and in thine hand it is to make great, and to give strength unto all. Now therefore, our God, we thank thee, and praise thy glorious name".

Do you have a testimony that glorifies God Almighty?

When was the last time you blessed the Lord God with your testimony?

I believe Pastors stopped testimony service because the Saints were talking about the devil more than they were giving God glory.

What would happen if during your next fellowship service at church, you got up and glorified God? You, telling of God's goodness and His faithfulness.

I believe it would stir the hearts of the listeners and they would take inventory, of just how great God is.

In Mark 11:23, Jesus let us know that we will have whatsoever we say.

Make prayer, praise, and glorifying God top priority in your life.

This is Testifying Monday.

MY PSALM TO MY KING

Psalm 45:1 AMPC
MY HEART overflows with a goodly theme; I address my
psalm to my King. My tongue is like the pen of a ready writer.

Praise to You O Lord my God. I see Your handy work and it's
marvelous in my eyes. I wake to new mercies and I'm grateful
for Your Grace. You're mindful of me that you created Calla
lilies just for me. I love your green grass and your clear blue
skies. Who is like You, O Lord? I've searched all over and I
can't find anyone like thee, O Lord of lords. You breathed in
my direction and now blessings overtake me like wine flowing
down mountains and hills. Your blessing is better than a
thousand kisses. Your touch is better than a million dollars in
the bank. Your love for me is never ending. You hand-picked
me and found great pleasure in doing so. Your tender mercies
come to me, so I live; For Your law is my delight. My heart is
filled with love and thanksgiving because You are my Father
and King, and I want for nothing. For You, O Most High,
supply all my need and grant me my desires. Thank You for
Your compassion and faithfulness to me. I love You, O God
Eternal.

Take time and write a Psalm to God O Most High

DO WHAT YOU MUST DO

In the book of Ezra, the children of Israel were in captivity in Babylon. In chapter 8 they were released and Ezra was leading them back home to Jerusalem. But a major problem arose.

Be honest. Have you ever encountered major problems, roadblocks, or difficulties since you been a believer?

Ezra was leading a nation and with all the excitement in the air, he forgot about the cities they had to travel through to get to Jerusalem.

In the land between Babylon and Jerusalem there were well known bands of robbers and thieves. Ezra had just told the King, "The hand of our God is upon all them for good that seek him; but his power and his wrath is against all them that forsake him" (V.22). In other words, Ezra told the King, "We don't need your help. Our God is good and He will protect and provide for us". But then reality set in.

Have you ever talked big in your faith and then when it came to stepping out in faith, reality set in?

I'll raise my hand to that. I've been there.

But then Ezra did what we as believers need to do more often, Called for a FAST.
V. 21. Then I proclaimed a fast there, at the river of Ahava, that we might afflict ourselves before our God, to seek of him a right way for us, and for our little ones, and for all our substance.

Maybe you're going through a similar situation and you need God's guidance. You must do what need to be done. FAST

Turn that plate down. Turn the TV off. Get off of Facebook. Turn off your phone. Consecrate yourself with prayer and fasting. Let God know how much you need Him. And watch God show up and show out.

Ezra 8:23 NLT
So we fasted and earnestly prayed that our God would take care of us, and he heard our prayer.

If God did it back then, He can do it again just for you.

Ezra 8:31
Then we departed from the river of Ahava on the twelfth day of the first month, to go unto Jerusalem: and the hand of our God was upon us, and he delivered us from the hand of the enemy, and of such as lay in wait by the way.

When we deny ourselves and seek God, we let Him know, "LORD, I need you".

We must do what we must do, to show God, we are depending totally on Him for our deliverance, breakthrough, healing, blessing, and miracle.

I encourage you, do what you must do.

STAND

Galatians 5:1
Stand fast therefore in the liberty wherewith Christ hath made us free, and be not entangled again with the yoke of bondage.

As I write this devotion, I'm also dealing with a bloody nose.

Please don't take this wrong, but once I settled down to hear from God Holy Spirit, blood started flowing from my nose.

But while it's flowing, I hear God Holy Spirit saying, "STAND".

The above scripture came to mind with so many others once I heard "STAND". I'm placing emphasis on STAND because God Holy Spirit emphasized, "STAND".

Don't go back to the way you use to think. You have the Mind of Christ.

Don't stress out over that which you see. Stay focused on the Cross.

Stand, when everyone else gives up. Stand, even if you have to stand alone. Stand, upon God's promises. Stand, when you've done everything else. STAND!!!!

Faith goes beyond speaking. In Mark 9:23 Jesus said, "If thou canst believe, all things are possible to him that believeth."

I BELIEVE!!!!!!!

I thank God Almighty that I have on my armour. No matter where I go, my armour is intact.

Ephesians 6:11,13-14
Put on the whole armour of God, that ye may be able to stand against the wiles of the devil. Wherefore take unto you the whole armour of God, that ye may be able to withstand in the evil day, and having done all, to stand. Stand therefore, having your loins girt about with truth, and having on the breastplate of righteousness;

When the enemy launches an attack we must counterattack with God's Word, Prayer, Praise, and Standing in FAITH.

Rather than being discouraged, I'm encouraged because I know there is GLORY after this.

This also let me know, my persistence in prayer is paying off because I struck the enemy's nerve. Oh yes. Hallelujah

To God be ALL GLORY

1 Corinthians 16:13 NLT
Be on guard. Stand firm in the faith. Be courageous. Be strong.

Job 37:14
Hearken unto this, O Job: stand still, and consider the wondrous works of God.

Now that the enemy know, his plans, plots, tactics, fiery darts, and all his evil foolishness is aborted in the incubator of his thought process, the bleeding has stopped.

Hallelujah

No matter what you go through, STAND.
Be determined to hold fast to your confession of FAITH.
STAND on God's Word and you will have the victory and God Almighty will get the Glory.

STAND

YOU HAVE THE VICTORY

There are so many scriptures that start off with pain, tragedies, and in need of healing but then JESUS steps into the picture and speak.

Mark 9:17-27 tell of the boy with the dumb spirit that kept casting him into the fire and the waters, but that spirit smartened up when it felt the presence of our King, Jesus The Anointed. The Carnal man couldn't cast this spirit out but Jesus our risen Lord and Savior told the spirit what to do. "Thou dumb and deaf spirit, I charge thee, come out of him, and enter no more into him."

Jesus has all power over all spirits.

Hallelujah. There's nothing too hard for our LORD.

In Luke 7:12, a widow woman was on her way to bury her only son. Jesus was also passing through the same area. Jesus saw this and had compassion. He stopped the funeral processional and spoke life into the dead boy's body. The boy sat up.

Jesus has power over death.

The enemy want to make us think that he has the last word. But don't you believe that nonsense. God has the final word.

When the disciples were on the boat and the wind and sea was raging, they called on JESUS. Jesus woke up, rebuked the wind and said to the sea, "Peace be still" (Mark 4:39). The raging winds and seas did what He said. They had to obey the KING of KINGS.

The storms in your life, will make you think they control you, but do like the disciples...call on Jesus.

2 Corinthians 2:14
Now thanks be unto God, which always causeth us to triumph

No matter the situation or circumstance, YOU HAVE THE VICTORY.

Isaiah 25:8
He will swallow up death in victory; and the Lord God will wipe away tears from off all faces; and the rebuke of his people shall he take away from off all the earth: for the Lord hath spoken it.

1 Corinthians 15:57
But thanks be to God, which giveth us the victory through our Lord Jesus Christ.

1 John 5:4
For whatsoever is born of God overcometh the world: and this is the victory that overcometh the world, even our faith.

Come on and sing with me.

Victory is mine, Victory is mine
Victory today is mine. I told Satan get thee behind. Victory today is mine.

Do you believe it
Do you believe that you have the VICTORY?
Well act like it.

Straighten up your crown of favor on your head.
Pull your shoulders back.
Push your chest out.
Now walk like you have the VICTORY.

You are victorious because you are the King's kid.
You have the VICTORY.

CAST IT ALL

To cast is to throw with force in a specific direction.

Have you ever cast something?

In 1 Peter 5:7 AMPC, Apostle Peter encourages all believers by telling them, "Casting the whole of your care all your anxieties, all your worries, all your concerns, once and for all on Him, for He cares for you affectionately and cares about you watchfully."

I join in with Apostle Peter, encouraging you to throw all your cares, concerns, and worries on God Almighty. He never sleeps nor slumber, and since He's going to be up all night, let Him deal with it so you can rest.

There's nothing God our Father won't do for you. His children are the most important part of His day. He's thinking about YOU!!!

Jeremiah 29:11 NKJV
For I know the thoughts that I think toward you, says the LORD, thoughts of peace and not of evil, to give you a future and a hope.

The Saints of old use to sing a song, "Turn it over to Jesus. He'll work it out".

That's what you need to do. Step out in faith and turn it, throw it, cast it, over to Jesus.

Today's Prayer:
Father God in Jesus Christ, I cast all my cares, concerns, worries, and anxieties on you. Father, cover me with Your strength, peace, wisdom, and spirit today and forever more. Help me overcome my unbelief.
And it is so. In Jesus Christ I pray. So be it unto me.

I pray that every word of this God Holy Spirit inspired book have encouraged and strengthened you in the Faith. My desire is that every believer fulfill their God given destiny as they minister to the loss about God's redeeming LOVE.

I decree blessings, favor, healing, and total wholeness in your life and in the lives of your seed.

Until my next book, enjoy the blessings of the Lord God Almighty.

In His Service,

Evangelist Lolita' M. Jones, MCJ, MFS.
USN, Ret.

The presence of the Lord, is sought in the inner chambers of the heart. Who are you seeking?

LIFE CHANGERS MINISTRIES

PRAYER LINE

JOIN OUR WEEKLY
EARLY MORNING PRAYER

EVERY MONDAY AT 6 AM EST/5 AM CST/ 3 AM PST

CONFERENCE NUMBER: (712) 775-7031
CODE:543530#

When thou saidst, Seek ye my face; my heart
said unto thee, Thy face, Lord, will I seek.
Psalm 27:8

HOST

EVANGELIST LOLITA' M. JONES

LIFELINE OF AMERICA
TOUCH AND AGREE
PRAYER LINE

JOIN US FOR CORPORATE PRAYER

MONDAY – FRIDAY
7 A.M.

1-303-536-1742

Verily, verily, I say unto you, He that believeth on me, the works that I do shall he do also; and greater works than these shall he do; because I go unto my Father. John 14:12

HOST
ELDER MICHAEL HARRIS

Made in the USA
Columbia, SC
13 December 2020